HOW TO START A CHILD CARE BUSINESS

A BEGINNER'S BLUEPRINT TO LAUNCHING AND GROWING A CHILD CARE BUSINESS INTO A PROFITABLE ENTERPRISE

AMELIA THOMPSON

CONTENTS

CHAPTER 1

TYPES OF CHILDCARE BUSINESSES

This chapter describes popular childcare service models—from commercial centers to in-home daycares and niche variations—comparing program structures, regulations, start-up costs and pros and cons of each approach. Aspiring owners can evaluate options to determine the ideal model aligning with their vision, skills and community needs.

Daycare Centers

Daycare centers are dedicated childcare facilities that provide care and supervision for infants through school-aged children. They operate during standard daytime business hours and do not provide overnight care. Daycare centers range greatly in size and may care for as few as 6 children up to 200+ children depending on the physical space and licensing regulations in their state.

Hours of Operation

Most daycare centers are open 12 or more hours per day, starting as early as 6 AM and closing at 6 or 7 PM. Common operating hours enable parents to drop off children before work in the morning and pick them up after traditional work hours. Some centers offer part-time enrollment options with shorter hours for parents who work non-traditional shifts or have alternative childcare plans certain days of the week.

While hourly drop-in care is not typically available at daycare centers, most centers establish set weekly or monthly enrollment schedules. This helps ensure appropriate teacher-to-child ratios are maintained at all times based on predicted attendance.

Ages Accepted

Daycare centers have the ability to accept children ranging from 6 weeks old once a baby is weaned from breast milk or formula and is able to take a bottle up to 5 or 6 years old when a child transitions into elementary school.

Infants and toddlers may be separated into their own classrooms overseen by teachers specialized in their unique developmental stages. Especially in larger centers, it is common to then have dedicated preschool rooms for 3-4 year olds focused on promoting kindergarten readiness through structured learning activities.

Teacher-to-Child Ratios

Maintaining appropriate teacher-to-child ratios is imperative for daycares to ensure adequate supervision, meet licensing standards, and operate safely and efficiently. While regulations differ slightly state-to-state, general nationwide standards are:

- Infants (6 weeks - 1 year): 1 teacher to 3-4 infants
- Toddlers (1 - 2 years): 1 teacher to 4-5 toddlers
- Twos: 1 teacher to 5-6 two year olds
- Preschoolers (3 - 5 years): 1 teacher to 10 - 12 preschoolers
- School Agers: 1 teacher to 15 - 20 school age children

Some states may have slightly higher caps on ratios but exceeding these averages often overburdens staff and compromises care, so most centers choose to stick to these general industry guidelines.

Classroom Structure

Classrooms in daycare centers are thoughtfully designed to promote learning and exploration in a safe environment. Each room addresses key developmental domains through a variety of toys, materials, and activities:

Infant Rooms focus heavily on movement skills and sensory development with open spaces for tummy time, mirrors, soft textures, graspable toys, and baby gyms. Diapering stations, cribs/mats for napping, and storage for bottles, formula, and food are essential.

Toddler Rooms enable freedom to walk/run with toys for gross motor development, sensory tables for tactile exploration, toys to enhance fine motor skills, and pictures/colors/shapes to stimulate visual learning. Potties and diaper stations are still needed as children potty train.

Preschool Rooms divide into learning centers such as dramatic play areas with costumes/puppets, library corners full of books, sensory bins for hands-on learning, writing centers for pre-literacy skills, block areas to encourage building, and tables for arts/crafts projects. Labels with pictures, letters, and numbers are posted throughout the room.

School Age Spaces revolve around opportunities for collaborative play and often mimic elementary classrooms with desks, academic games that reinforce math/reading skills, and spaces for building or loose parts play.

Sample Daily Schedules

While flexibility is necessary when caring for young children, centers establish predictable daily routines to provide consistency and structure. Here is an overview of common schedules that may be adapted across age groups:

Morning Routine (7 - 9 AM)

- Free choice centers/arrival activities
- Hand washing and breakfast
- Circle time with songs, stories, calendar, weather

Mid-Morning (9 - 11:30 AM)

- Learning centers (arts/crafts, science, sensory play, fine/gross motor skills)
- Large group activities
- Outdoor or gym play

Lunch (11:30 AM - 12:30 PM)

- Hand washing and lunch
- Quiet reading time while children finish eating

Nap/Rest Time (12:30 - 2:30 PM)

- Quiet calming activities for non-nappers
- Nap/rest for children under 5
- Movie or board games for school age

Afternoon (2:30 - 6 PM)

- Snack time
- Resume learning centers
- Small group enrichment activities
- Outdoor/gym play
- Departure routine

This predictable flow enhances security while allowing wiggle room to shape activities around children's interests each day.

Transportation

Unlike preschool programs which provide dedicated busing, most daycare centers do not offer transportation to/from their facilities. Parents or guardians are responsible for dropping off and picking up children during established operating hours.

However, some larger centers with ample outdoor space or in rural areas may opt to purchase daycare vans. These buses enable teachers to transport groups of children on local field trips to community parks, zoos, children's museums and other nearby attractions to supplement in-house learning. All drivers undergo training and criminal background checks before operating vehicles.

Meals and Snacks

Since children are present for long hours, most daycare centers provide breakfast, lunch and afternoon snacks catered around nap schedules. Meals adhere to USDA standards supporting healthy growth and development. Infant feeding aligns with parents' requests whether breast milk, formula, or solid foods.

For older children, meals incorporate essential food groups with fruits, vegetables, proteins and whole grains. Snacks often include yogurt, crackers/pretzels and raisins. Accommodations address documented allergies and dietary needs. Some centers partner with catering companies while others have full kitchens and hire cooks to prepare well-balanced kids' menus.

Accreditation

When researching daycare centers, look for accreditation through the National Association for the Education of Young Children (NAEYC). This rigorous accreditation process promotes best practices related to health, safety, nutrition, teacher training, diversity, community relationships and early learning. NAEYC accreditation provides parents assurance their children receive high quality care and education during formative developmental years.

Preschools

Preschools provide early childhood education for children too young to enter kindergarten, typically ages 3-5. They operate during daytime hours mirroring elementary school schedules and do not offer childcare services beyond several hours per day. Many preschools align with traditional academic calendars from September through May.

Hours of Operation

Most preschool programs run on 4 or 5 day per week schedules with set part-day or full-day options. Half day programs generally operate for 2.5 to 3.5 hours either in the morning or afternoon. Full day options extend up to 6 hours daily. Parents can choose enrollment schedules ranging from just 2 mornings per week up to 5 full days depending on family needs and budgets.

While preschools do not provide childcare per se, some offer pre/post care to accommodate working parents. This extended supervision time enables earlier drop-offs before class and/or later pickups after dismissal for an added fee.

Ages Accepted

Preschools primarily accept children 3-4 years old but may take younger 2.5 year olds who turn 3 during that academic year. Children are expected to be fully potty trained before starting.

Many preschools are play-based to nurture development while others focus more heavily on structured learning for pre-academic skill building depending on educational philosophies. Some preschools even blend together children nearing kindergarten readiness with younger students to enable peer modeling.

Teacher-to-Child Ratios

In order to facilitate learning and meet licensing criteria, preschool programs maintain small class sizes with one lead teacher overseeing assistant teachers and teacher aids. Common preschool ratios are:

- 1 teacher to 10 children
- 1 teacher + 1 assistant teacher to 16 children
- 1 teacher + 2 assistants to 18 children

These small ratios allow teachers to get to know each child

individually and cater to varying abilities as students grow socially, physically and intellectually.

Classroom Design

Preschool classrooms intentionally nurture key developmental domains through a variety of centers, materials and hands-on activities. Dramatic play areas let children role play occupations while developing verbal skills. Puppet theaters and costumes stimulate self-expression.

Library corners are full of books to enhance pre-literacy skills and foster a love of reading. Writing centers with paper, stencils and crayons help strengthen fine motor control needed for eventually gripping pencils correctly. Math manipulatives like counting beads, puzzles and blocks build early numerical recognition.

Sensory tables allow discovery through sand, rice, water or other media. Science stations share magnifying glasses, magnets, seashells and specimens to inspect. Many classrooms have fish tanks or butterfly gardens to learn life cycles. Art centers reinforce creativity and dexterity with varying art mediums from paint to playdough.

Curriculum Standards

While playing games like Duck Duck Goose or Red Light Green Light, children develop gross motor skills, learn to listen and follow multi-step directions. Circle time reinforces numbers, letters, colors, patterns and rhyming through stories, finger plays and music. Free choice time enables exploration through different domains at self-directed paces.

Most states outline Early Learning Standards or Guidelines that structure preschool learning objectives across multiple domains:

- Physical Wellbeing & Motor Development: gross/fine motor skills, healthy practices
- Social & Emotional Development: self-awareness,

self-regulation, social awareness, relationship skills
- Approaches to Learning: curiosity, initiative, persistence, creativity, reasoning
- Language & Literacy: communication, pre-reading skills, comprehension, vocabulary
- Cognition & General Knowledge: memory, problem solving, counting, shapes, sorting
- Subject Matter Concepts: science, social studies, arts, technology

Lessons connect across disciplines to reinforce skills through repetition in meaningful contexts. Assessment tracks development to identify needs.

Daily Schedules

Here is an example full-day preschool schedule:
- Arrival/Check-In (8:00 - 8:30 AM) - Hang backpacks and coats, wash hands, bathroom, table toys
- Circle Time (8:30 - 9 AM) - Welcome song, calendar, theme introduction
- Learning Centers (9 - 10 AM) -Rotation through art, science, writing, math and puzzles
- Clean Up/Snack (10 - 10:30 AM)
- Story Time (10:30 - 11 AM) - Read books, comprehension questions
- Outside Play (11 AM - 12 PM)
- Lunch (12 - 1 PM)
- Nap/Quiet Time (1 - 2:30 PM) - Yoga, calming music
- Group Activity (2:30 - 3 PM) - Cooperative games, movement, acting
- Learning Centers (3 - 4 PM)
- Pack Up/Departure (4 - 4:30 PM)

Consistent routines provide structure while flexibility caters to teachable moments. Field trips, special guests (firefighters, dentists) and holiday parties enrich standard curriculum.

Transportation & Meals

Unlike daycare centers, most preschools do not provide transportation or meals. Parents drop off/pick up children before/after class sessions. Some may offer lunch programs or snacks provided by parents on a rotating schedule. Accommodations address any food allergies.

Those with extended hours may serve light morning/afternoon snacks. But the shorter academic portions of the day do not warrant full meal preparation. Sometimes catered lunch options can be purchased for full-day sessions.

Accreditation

When researching preschools, look for accreditation through the National Association for the Education of Young Children (NAEYC) which indicates programs meet rigorous standards related to early childhood curriculum quality, teacher qualifications, health and safety procedures, and family involvement.

In-Home Daycares

In-home daycares provide childcare out of a licensed provider's private residence for a small group of children. Since they operate out of a home rather than a commercial facility, in-home daycares offer convenient neighborhood access and often charge lower rates than larger centers. They give children a comfortable, "home away from home" environment while parents work.

Hours of Operation

Most in-home daycares are open standard full-time business hours from around 6 AM to 6 PM Monday through Friday. Some providers may limit hours from 8 AM - 4 PM if they have flexibility from spouses, older children, or other income. Hours must be reliable for parents' commuting needs.

While primarily operating on a standard weekly schedule, some in-home providers offer parents flexibility for drop-in care on an emergency or as-needed basis which larger centers don't allow. These flexible hours appeal to shift workers like nurses who have changing schedules.

Ages Accepted

In-home daycares generally accept children from infants 6 weeks old up through 6 years when children enter elementary school. The small groups enable mixing of ages through toddler years until children shift into preschool curriculum around ages 3-5.

Some providers start by exclusively caring for infants and expand up through toddlers. Others focus only on 2-5 year old preschool ages. Most accept complete age ranges in order to sustain long-term enrollment keeping children year after year.

Teacher-to-Child Ratios

In-home daycares maintain smaller mixed age groupings than commercial centers, although limits on number served depend upon state licensing categories. These categories align with teacher-to-child ratios:

- Small - max of 6 children
- Medium - max of 10-12 children
- Large - max of 16 children

Helpers like spouses or substitutes can briefly assist allowing providers to care for additional children beyond regular ratios. But generally ratios align with licensing caps which determine enrollment limits.

Environment

In-home daycares repurpose private residential spaces to meet licensing safety standards for young children. Providers childproof homes covering outlets, securing cabinets, gating stairs and removing choking hazards. Play areas partition off living spaces while still feeling homey.

Key environmental features include:

- Baby proofed play spaces
- Diapering stations
- Nap mat/cot storage
- Children's restrooms, sinks and toilets
- Bottles, formula and solid food prep areas
- Learning materials, toys and arts supplies
- Secured outdoor play areas
- First aid kits and safety tools
- Child proofed vehicles with car seats

While not mimicking full commercial center infrastructure, in-home daycares offer play kitchens, sensory tables, age-appropriate toys, arts supplies, dress-up clothes and train sets fostering learning through play. Outdoor swing sets, playhouses, water tables and riding toys develop gross motor skills. Both educational and nurturing, home environments often feel like a big, loving family.

Sample Daily Schedule

Here's a typical schedule in an in-home daycare:

Morning Routine (7 - 9 AM)

- Free play
- Diapering/potty
- Breakfast
- Learning centers

Mid-Morning (9 - 11 AM)

- Arts & crafts
- Circle time (songs, stories, fingerplays)
- Outdoor play

Lunch (11 AM - 12 PM)

- Diapering/potty
- Meal time

Nap Time (12 - 2:30 PM)

- Storytime
- Rest/quiet time
- Quiet activities for non-nappers

Afternoon (2:30 - 6 PM)

- Snack time
- Sensory play
- Indoor physical activities
- Learning centers/enrichment
- Outdoor play
- Departures

While this schedule provides an overview, actual timing remains flexible catering to children's moods and needs each day. Providers balance nurturing care with kindergarten readiness.

Transportation & Meals

Unless taking walking field trips, parents provide transportation to/from in-home daycares. Some providers utilize daycare vans to enable local excursions to parks, libraries or toddler gyms. Vehicles have car seats with regular maintenance and inspections.

Since children may attend 9 hours or longer, in-home daycares provide breakfast, lunch and PM snacks. Many menus align with USDA guidelines for childhood nutrition. Providers are trained in infant bottle prep, introducing first foods and meal safety. They address allergies, dietary restrictions and permit parents to bring breastmilk. Some states mandate special menus for those claiming "healthful" food.

Accreditation

No national accreditation currently exists for in-home

daycares; however, most states establish licensing criteria addressing health, safety, nutrition, caregiver training, facility standards and learning materials. Carefully review state regulations when evaluating quality indicators for in-home providers. Ask about background checks, first aid/CPR certification, substitutes, and liability insurance. Ensure excellent communication fits your family's needs.

Nanny Services

A nanny provides personalized care for children inside a family's private residence. As integral household members, nannies give dedicated solo attention meeting all parenting needs from nurturing infants to facilitating learning activities for older kids. Nanny services offer completely customized schedules and care tailored towards individual children.

Hours & Schedules

Nannies work flexible full-time or part-time hours based solely around families' unique needs. Live-in nannies reside in the home for extended durations. They get evenings, weekends and overnight off per agreements while remaining on-call other times. Live-out nannies commute to the residence during agreed upon daytime hours.

Typical nanny needs range from:

- Full weekday coverage for parents who work outside the home
- Mornings getting kids ready and to school
- After-school care including driving to activities
- Overnight help when parents travel for work
- Back-up care when primary childcare falls through
- Weekend childcare assistance

Nannies provide whatever support families require during employment periods from a few months up to years consistently caring for children as they grow.

Ages Served

Nannies care for all ages of children from newborns through teenage years. Infant care specialists have expertise meeting all developmental and safety needs of babies 0-12 months old. Other nannies prefer interacting with verbal toddlers and preschool ages teaching colors, shapes and ABCs. Still others feel confident managing school drop-offs/pick-ups for elementary ages through middle schoolers assisting with homework.

Nanny ages skew slightly older than other childcare teachers given the independent responsibility carrying for children without additional staff on premises. Maturity and substantial experience calm parents' concerns regarding extensive solo time babysitting in private households while parents are occupied or absent.

Nanny-to-Child Ratio

The nanny directly cares for the contracted number of children in a family without supervision or assistance from other adults. While ratios in commercial daycares regulate teacher workloads, nannies give individualized attention. It is common for one nanny to care for:

- 1-3 children in a single family
- Up to 4 children if older siblings help entertain one another
- Infant multiples like twins or triplets

Nannies interact, play games, supervise meals, orchestrate naps and drive children wherever needed each day to keep kids safe and happily engaged. Adjustments accommodate sick days needing extra cuddles or hectic schedules shuffling multiple kids in various directions.

Environmental Set-Up

Nannies utilize existing play areas, toys and baby equipment within family homes while parents are away. Employers commonly designate spaces for the nanny to facilitate play and learning during designated work hours.

Items like arts/crafts, dress-ups, train sets and reading nooks entertain multiple ages at once while containing mess.

Parents provide all necessary gear including:

- Bassinets, cribs, beds
- Highchairs and booster seats
- Strollers and baby carriers
- Car seats
- Baby gates, cabinet locks and outlet covers
- Age appropriate toys
- Outdoor play equipment
- Electronic baby monitors/video cameras

Nannies keep children safe utilizing dedicated resources while parents manage environmental set-ups. Some bring additional activities bags, craft supplies or worksheet packets. But supervision happens utilizing children's personal spaces and belongings.

Sample Nanny Work Day

A typical nanny shift involves continuous interaction caring for and playing with children all hours of the day. Nannies perform all parental duties like feeding, bathing, dressing, diapering infants or directly supervising older kids' self-care. Activities entertain tiny ones learning to crawl up through teens who need reminders to complete school assignments.

Here's an example nanny schedule for toddler and preschooler:

- 6:30 AM - Wake up, breakfast, get dressed
- 8 AM – Playtime while tidying up kitchen
- 9 AM - Outdoor walk or playground
- 10 AM - Arts & crafts project
- 11 AM - Lunch prep and eating
- 12 PM - Storytime then nap

- 2 PM – Snack then playtime
- 3:30 PM - Scholar workbooks
- 5 PM – Clean up toys and dinner prep
- 6:15 PM - Parents return home

Schedules cater around parents' hours, children's moods and household needs with endless energy and attentiveness.

Excursions & Transportation

Nannies become extensions of parents chauffeuring children wherever needed using family vehicles. Nannies take children to pediatrician visits, gymnastics practice, friend's birthday parties and school. Using appropriate car restraints, they carefully transport kids of all ages across town on public roadways.

Nannies also facilitate local excursions to zoos, parks, museums and libraries so kids learn about their community. Stroller walks provide infants exercise and stimulation. Having another adult permits safer adventuring matching busy energy levels of active toddlers and preschoolers.

Meals & Snacks

Nannies nourish kids throughout the day preparing bottles, meals, snacks on scheduled intervals. Employers provide enough infant formula, solid baby foods purees or toddler snacks to sustain hungry children. Nannies keep kids hydrated and nourished, encouraging self-feeding as motor skills progress.

For older children, nannies fix simple snacks, heat up pre-made meals or follow written instructions to assemble daily lunches. They ensure kids eat enough fruits, protein and vegetables meeting unique dietary or allergy needs. Used dishes get handwashed or loaded into household dishwashers afterwards.

Credentials

When seeking nannies, ensure candidates complete background checks, CPR/first aid training, coaching in early childhood development milestones and have childcare references available. Many career nannies pursue formal credentials taking college classes in elementary/special education. Top sites like Care.com indicate verified identification, passing safety exams and years of experience.

Babysitting Co-ops

Babysitting co-ops (also called cooperatives) are networks of family members and neighborhood parents who take turns watching one another's children for free in order to save on childcare costs and trade services. They provide community goodwill facilitating adult social connections along with overseeing play for kids of similar ages.

Function

Members of a babysitting co-op typically live near one another or share community gathering places like schools, recreational centers and places of worship. By taking turns hosting at personal homes during evenings/weekends or meeting at common parks in nice weather, trusted adults within the co-op supervise member kids allowing parents to run errands and get work done.

The shared service structure depends upon parents contributing as much time babysitting other families' children to earn the hours of care they utilize from others. Tracking logistics vary - some co-ops use apps or spreadsheets tallying hours while more casual versions simply depend on the honor system with members informally estimating equitable exchanges.

Hours

Most babysitting co-ops outline rules determining length of time children can be left ranging from 2 hours to 4 hours per family per day. Some designate hours relative to number of kids being watched - for example 1 child = 2 hours but 2+ kids = 4 hours total. Families rank frequency of need from occasional to unlimited with member voting approving limits.

Member parents might utilize co-op babysitting for:
Weekly errand time
Medical appointments
Date nights
Gym workout sessions
Housecleaning or bill pay
Nap time for parents of infants
Quiet work hours

Co-ops only accommodate short durations, not all day or overnight needs. But the free, reliable care provides enough flexibility for parenting obligations.

Kids' Ages

Most babysitting co-ops start with members having kids under age 2 up through around 8 before tweens become more independent. Infants often combine with mobile toddlers and early preschool ages at first, eventually expanding into early elementary years as babies grow together. Older kids can then help entertain each other with less hands-on supervision needed.

Some groups accommodate nursing newborns carrying them along if mothers interchange babysitting shifts right away. Guidelines ensure caregiver-to-child ratios stay reasonable depending on ages. Facilities work best for young ages - parks for preschool/elementary kids but houses for infants and toddlers needing diapers, naps and bottle feedings on site.

Teacher-to-Child Ratios

Member parents serve as substitute caregivers whenever overseeing the co-op's children. Depending on ages, one hosting parent at their home typically oversees:

- 2-3 infants wearing baby monitors
- 4-5 toddlers contained in a childproof area
- 6-8 preschoolers engaged in play or crafts
- 10-12 school age kids playing games

Those amounts keep adult-to-child ratios manageable considering parents rotate these duties rather than possessing professional teaching skills. Some parents bring their own kids along to maintain eyes simultaneously on both families' children.

Facilities

Member families open up private residences for babysitting shifts using whatever play areas or toys they already own for personal kids. Host sites utilize baby gates, playpens and childproofing to keep rooms secure for visiting little ones on site. Preschool activities like playdough, sensory tables, train sets and dress-ups engage young minds if boredom sets in. Sites stock changing tables, high chairs or booster seats as needed.

For cooperative gatherings at member houses, Frequently parents arrange adjoining play in living rooms for infants alongside kitchens or basements occupied by older kids rotated every 2 hours. Nice weather permits all ages relocating together at shared playgrounds too. Sites must offer cleanliness, adequate supervision and safety checks.

Sample Babysitting Shifts

A typical 2-3 hour babysitting co-op shift might align with the following schedule:

0-60 minutes: Free play or playground time as kids arrive to burn energy

60-90 minutes: Snack time then craft project, sensory play, or reading stories

90-120 minutes: Nap for little ones or movie for ages 3-5

Final 60 minutes: Pack up time - Clean up toys, arts & crafts then parents pick up kids

The routine allows flexibility if infants need bottles or naps while older ones play. Timings approximate although pickup should occur before fatigue or boredom sets in.

Transportation

Babysitting co-ops only work for members in close proximity who can transport kids to/from residential member homes or mutually agreed upon parks. Parents drop children off, then retrieve the kids they enrolled at appointed ending times. Codes of conduct prohibit teenage members from driving other families' young children. Licensed adult members commute their own kids both directions.

Food Rules

Parents pre-feed children or supply snacks to avoid food sharing and allergic reactions. Some co-ops vote only allowing factory sealed snacks like goldfish crackers or apple sauce versus homemade goods. Clear ingredient labels give clarity if dietary restrictions exist. Providing own water bottles or sippy cups also prevents illness transmission.

Any meals must be fully nut-free if severe allergies exist in the group. Parents get updates if kids reject bottles or snacks to relay hunger signals. Good hygiene and cleaning regimen prevent contamination in facilities, toys, seats or bedding too.

Vetting Members

While not extensively regulated entities, most babysitting co-ops share member rosters publicly listing kids names, ages and policy agreement. Friend or acquaintance referrals confirm potential new joiner's reputations. Some groups limit eligibility to attendees of a house of worship. Startup meetings allow members to mutually assess sensible age alignments and trustworthiness. Annual dues or start fees discourage flighty participants prioritizing reliability.

Overnight/24-Hour Care

Overnight and 24-hour childcare facilities enable parents who work non-traditional hours, travel frequently away from home overnight, or need round-the-clock care for other reasons to ensure their children remain protected and cared for at all times of day. These programs take over when standard daytime services end.

Hours of Operation

24-hour childcare centers operate 365 days per year, 7 days a week, opening in the early evening around 6 PM and closing the following morning around 7 AM. Some locations function like daycare centers settling kids into overnight routines through the evening then transitioning to standard daycare operations from morning through early evening. Staff work shifts handing off custody.

Other overnight centers run independently just covering evening through morning hours when traditional centers close. A few locations function as emergency drop-in sites with later evening and very early morning hours as needed outside routine childcare. Sites cater to varying work schedules with full 24/7 availability as parents' job demands ebb and flow.

Ages Accepted

Overnight care accepts children ranging from infancy up to age 12 with groupings and activities tailored appropriately to developmental stages. Infants and toddlers follow usual sleeping and feeding patterns. Preschoolers settle down with story times and air mattresses for resting. School-agers relax in pajamas with movie nights after homework help.

Some overnight facilities skew towards teenage care tying programming to recreational sports, field trips, mentoring and counseling for vulnerable youth. But most strive to serve all ages needing reliable supervision while parents handle jobs or other obligations.

Staff-to-Child Ratios

To ensure proper supervision overnight, facilities maintain similar teacher-to-child ratios following best practices as daycares:

- Infants - 1:3 or 1:4
- Toddlers - Up to 1:5
- Preschoolers - 1:7 or 1:10

- School Age - At least 1:12

Some states mandate lower caps on school-agers in overnight facilities allowing only 1:8. Regulations require at least 2 adults present at all times for safety with more added based on occupancy and ages served. Small groups keep kids secure late into the night.

Environment

Overnight centers alter traditional programmatic spaces facilitating children's sleep schedules and hygiene needs into the late hours. Infants sleep in separate rooms in cribs with staff checking on them around the clock as needed for feedings and diaper changes. Security cameras monitor rooms and hallways. Toddlers and preschoolers wash up before getting cozy on cots or mats.

Low lighting sets moods after dinner time while lamps enable middle of the night checks or bottles. Soothing music and lullaby sounds relax restless children once settled into slumber aligned with usual bedtimes. Separate short-term overnight boarding facilitates parents traveling without children disrupting household sleep rhythms.

Evening Schedule

As children arrive in the evening staff engage them in play or quiet reading times winding down from the day. Younger groups take baths with fresh pajamas distinguishing nighttime routines from afternoon departure commotion. Around 8 PM dinner meals cater to enrollment with appropriately timed infant bottles. Per state licensing, no bottles occur laying down preventing ear infections.

One hour of educational play or crafts follows dinner to sustain enrichment without excessive stimulation before bed. Calm activities like light tables, sensory immersion, yoga or soft music channel students for maximum rest. By 10 PM staff involve teeth brushing and bathroom breaks before tucking preschoolers into nap mats or cribs using transitional objects like stuffed animals or blankets brought from home for comfort. Peaceful slumber ideally lasts 6+ hours as teachers supervise overnight.

Morning Schedule

Teachers gently wake children for bathroom breaks and diaper changes around 5 AM. Bottles serve babies first prioritizing their hunger cues. Around 6 AM breakfast foods like cereal, fruit and milk nourish toddlers, preschoolers and school-agers preparing them to resume standard programming once day centers reopen. Kids play or watch educational programming until daytime caregivers staff facilities again by 7 AM.

Transportation

Like traditional centers, most 24-hour facilities do not provide transportation to and from the overnight location. Contracted policies assume parents or approved guardians drop children off and pick them up again according to work shifts timing out custodial care needs. However, some partner with child protective agencies placing children in emergency overnight custody when necessary for safety plans. Case workers would commute kids as required in crisis situations when parents are incapable of doing so directly.

Nutrition

Since 24-hour programming essentially functions as both daycare and overnight boarding in one, kitchens remain fully operational nearly around the clock providing meals, snacks and formula on demand. State licensing commonly oversees menu quality and nutrition similar to daycare expectations. Providers store adequate food on-hand for on-demand feedings with refrigeration and warming capabilities overnight as needs arise unpredictable to staffing. Sleep transitions and hunger can spur spurts of eating at all hours.

Accreditation

When vetting 24 hour care, check if better business bureau

accreditation exists or partnerships with overnight boarding associations. Given round-the-clock services, more rigorous oversight and monitoring helps assure proper training, accountability and responsibility within a longer chain of custody. Ask about licensing, liability, staff turnover, contingency planning, and evidence handling. Look for superior cleanliness and orderliness during late night chaos. Assess comprehensive coverage qualifying caretakers for unpredictable duties amid challenging overnight timeframes. Prioritize locations nurturing comforts of home so children rest peacefully.

Special Needs Care

Special needs childcare centers and programs serve children who require developmental, medical, behavioral, communication or personal assistance intervention exceeding capabilities of standard daycare facilities. Extra staff training, accessibility accommodations, adaptive equipment and customized activities tailored to disabilities allow inclusive environments where unique kids thrive.

Common Diagnoses

Children benefitting from special needs programming may have diagnoses including:

- Autism Spectrum Disorders
- Sensory Processing Disorders
- Attention Deficit Hyperactivity Disorders
- Speech and language delays
- Down Syndrome
- Cerebral Palsy
- Spina Bifida
- Seizure Disorders like Epilepsy
- Childhood Cancers
- Diabetes
- Cystic Fibrosis

- Food Allergies

Care plans address challenges like social difficulties, impulse control, allergen risks, mobility assistance, medical procedures, behavioral redirection, sensory stimulation, restricted diets and developmental delays needing elevated professional intervention. Specially trained staff provide supplementary care supplementing any external therapies.

Hours of Operation

Most special needs programs run akin to preschool schedules operating 4-5 hours per weekday without extensive before/after school care or summer services. Some match elementary session timing to include transportation to/from public school special education classrooms for pre-academics. Others function more like respite care with flexible hourly drop-in rates to assist families managing exhausting caretaking off-shifts. Hours meet clinical realities since round-the-clock intervention easily burns out staff.

A few intensive treatment centers provide extensive full-time and even residential care for more severely involved kids. But commonly programs conserve student stamina spacing longer days over just 2-3 sessions per week. Supplemental private therapies then bolster learning. Weekends and holidays close to prevent staff fatigue and hefty overhead since supplemental funding sustains special needs programming challenging financial sustainability.

Staff-to-Child Ratios

To optimize highly customized instruction, special needs classrooms maintain lower teacher-to-student ratios than typical daycare regulations requiring:

- 1 teacher per 3-4 infants
- 1 teacher per 3-6 preschool students
- Tiered levels of 1 teacher per 3 up to 12 school-age kids depending on support needs

Additional classroom aides, therapists, school

psychologists, behavioral specialists and volunteers provide individuals robust professional attention as needs dictate. Adults continuously circulate addressing needs from medical intervention to emotional meltdowns to learning reinforcement.

Environment

Special needs classrooms adapt physical layouts to benefit differently-abled students via abundant floor spacing, guardrails and mobility ramps. Padded areas cushion accidental falls while soundproofing dampens noise sensitivities. Enclosed nooks become quiet retreats during overstimulation. Toy shelves sit at wheelchair heights enabling independence.

Visual schedules with pictures, symbols and colors structure procedures through posted step sequences. Calming colors avoid overstimulation. Sinks allow hand-over-hand washing help developing self-care skills. Specialized bathroom equipment assists toileting. Assistive communication devices aid nonverbal students while sign language displays reinforce verbal speech. Additional facilities accommodate feeding tubes, ostomy needs, injections, respiratory treatments and physical therapy exercises. Extensive gear storage houses mobility aids when not in use so rooms flex to activities. Outdoors, landscaping provides textured sensation paths and adaptable playgrounds developing motor skills.

Adapted Curriculum

Specialists adapt teaching strategies suiting individual capabilities through multi-sensory cueing using verbal narration reinforced visually via sign language, pictures and hands-on demonstrations. Less instruction rests solely auditory unlike general preschool story times. Activities break into incremental steps slowing pacing while extending time on task for mastery before sequencing together more complex skills.

For example, art projects require grip assistance holding markers to scratch lines on paper building towards eventual capability coloring shapes. Circle times involve songs with motions reinforcing shapes, letters and counting for math skills paired to physical movement. Positioning aids proper posture and mobility during floor play. Outdoor walks build community safety skills over time rather than immediately playground interactions. Baby steps towards goals scaffold success.

Speech therapists facilitate communication growth through physical mouth muscle strengthening exercises enabling verbal pronunciations. Occupational and physical therapists improve balance, coordination and strength key to manipulating toys or eating utensils. Goals intertwine improving cognitive, muscular, sensory and social abilities simultaneously.

Case Management & Family Resources

Given wide-ranging developmental and medical needs plus coordination ensuring comprehensive therapy coverage, special needs personnel act as case managers securing financial support, tracking lesson plans, data logging progress and adjusting accommodations. Staff aim to bolster family wellness and parenting confidence not just student benchmarks. Caregiver stress and emotional dynamics remain high priorities never overlooked during other goal setting.

Ongoing partnerships between center teams and parents/guardians mutually determine optimal achievement routes respecting diverse family values while expanding possibilities. Trusted guidance navigates overwhelming bureaucracy across healthcare and educational systems to access every benefit kids deserve. Support applies to parents facing grieving complex diagnoses, insurance denials or coping with strained relationships given high caretaking demands. Special needs care blends practical skill advancement and human compassion tailoring everything to exclusive child and family rhythms.

Accreditation & Credentials

When researching special needs programming, ask whether the Council for Exceptional Children accredits the center demonstrating quality standards for individualized curriculum, therapeutic inclusion and supportive technologies meeting unique learner needs. Also look for integrative staff possessing both early childhood and special education licenses able to dually nurture development while elevating capacities responding to disabilities shaping growth. Diversity training indicators further assure welcoming inclusive spaces embracing each child and family's journey.

Drop-In Centers

Drop-in childcare centers provide flexible, temporary supervision for families needing occasional care for a few hours without enrolling long-term. They serve as back-up options when regular arrangements fall through or parents require intermittent coverage for work obligations or errands. Most limit attendance from 1-4 hours at a time.

Function

Drop-in centers offer custodial oversight so parents tackle responsibilities when usual caregivers cannot cover. They alleviate stresses scrambling last minute when a babysitter cancels, school closes early, a business trip arises suddenly or mom gets stuck overtime at the office. For one low hourly rate and no recurring financial commitment, children receive safe short-term care including toys and activities.

Drop-in flexibility assists parents to address life's unpredictable demands without needing to miss work or drag kids on tedious errands. Some centers focus exclusively on emergency use while others encourage routine drop-ins for a change of scenery benefiting home-based daycares or isolated latchkey kids too. Most take walk-ins happily as capacity allows although reserving spots ensures availability when urgently needed most.

Hours

Drop-in centers commonly operate weekday hours from 8am until 6pm covering standard business days. Some locations extend earlier or later to enable commuting time for hectic, over-scheduled families on the go. Certain franchises stay open 24/7 to handle odd shifts or overnights in a pinch too. Hourly rates apply upon arrival and remain the same all sessions whether kids play 10 minutes or 2 hours.

Time limits prevent overstays although 2-4 hours suffices running essential errands. Hourly offerings contrast full-day childcare enabling parents focused bursts handling domestic needs. Some centers divide into partial or full day packages capping coverage limits at 4 hours versus 10. But no multi-day subscriptions apply so returns never feel obligatory after satisfying temporary supervision demands. Sign in, fulfill business, then promptly sign back out.

Ages Accepted

Most drop-in facilities cater to a wide span of ages from infancy through age 12 with partitioned spaces and programming designated by developmental stage. Infant rooms feature cribs, swings, and plush floor mats. Toddler zones contain sensory tables, building blocks and puzzles. An arts and crafts area occupies preschool kids with coloring stations. School-agers lounge around tables playing board games, reading books or drawing. Mixed ages rotate through common playgrounds under watchful supervision keeping everyone happily engaged but separated by appropriate skills.

Teacher-to-Child Ratios

In order to maintain orderly control despite unpredictable attendance fluctuations inherent to drop-in care, facilities strictly comply with or exceed state-mandated classroom ratios:

- Infants 1:3
- Toddlers 1:5
- Preschoolers 1:8
- School Age 1:10

Caregivers hold appropriate credentials to cover whichever ages drop in on any given day. Extra staff switches assignments as ratios tip through hourly arrivals and departures. At maximum occupancy, centers limit new registrations until existing children cycle out maintaining compliance.

Environment

Drop-in centers closely resemble traditional daycare facilities in smaller settings. Colorful wall murals, alphabetical rug squares and designated learning zones partition room space optimizing play for each age bracket. Infants relax in rockers or on activity gyms with soft hanging toys and mirrors. Toddlers sit in pint-sized chairs around playdough stations, toy kitchens and block areas. Preschoolers inhabit dress-up corners, sensory tables and toy workbenches. School-agers claim comfy beanbags for reading.

Separation allows groups developmental freedom tailored to abilities away from vulnerability issues with bigger kids yet shared hallways and communal playgrounds outside enable periodic interactions when desired developmentally. Extra staff continuously circulates redirecting activities if conflicts arise.

Structure

With unpredictable attendance, loose flow accommodates students' preferences optimizing limited hours on site. Check-in kiosks log arrivals electronically with pertinent info as parents scan access cards and register exact ages for proper classifications. Staff then ushers kids to pre-designated areas already equipped for age-appropriate play by interest while parents commence work or errands. Periodic games, songs and stories Rally group attention briefly.

During longer stays, scheduled meal times serve nutritionally balanced snacks or lunches if enrolled over lunch hours. Eventually parents return using ID cards to finalize accrued time and checkout children. Custom software tallies precise hourly charges deducting automatically from preloaded customer accounts. Quick attendants then tidy areas fully sanitizing all toys awaiting the next round of unanticipated attendees trickling in soon thereafter.

Transportation

Unlike daily childcare options, drop-in facilities do not transport kids to or from locations. The convenience relies fully on proximate parental drop off and pick up midday allowing independent task completion in between. Sites choose locations near business hubs, shopping centers, community centers or residential neighborhoods precisely so scattered parents access interim supervision along existing commute routes or daily trajectories without detouring far from pre-established errand completions or commuting patterns critical to households.

Parents tour facilities initially to verify agreeable care standards, policies and cleanliness firsthand. But subsequently assume all transportation directly during brief enrollment periods spanning only hours not months like subscription services. Approximate locations underpin the entire concept.

Nutrition

Given unpredictable and intermittent attendance patterns, drop-in centers lack kitchen infrastructure preparing well-balanced kids' meals from scratch. However they store nutritious pre-packaged snacks compliant with USDA childhood nutrition recommendations to dish out on-

31

demand if kids complain of hunger during longer stretches on site. Easy grab items like yogurt cups, apple sauce pouches, veggie straws, goldfish crackers, cereal bars and fruit snacks tide over kids temporarily without spoiling later appetites for family dinner.

Water dispensers provide continual access to hydration as well. Parents pack clearly labeled Sippy cups or water bottles avoiding potential sharing germs with unknown parties frequenting common areas episodically who never enroll long enough to track health histories. Simple shelf stable foods suffice meeting intermittent community needs reasonably without attempting elaborate catering feats.

Accreditation

Standalone drop-in facilities rarely pursue accreditation through national childcare excellence programs considering their limited hours of operation, constantly fluctuating enrollment and inability to thoroughly evaluate long-ranging child advancement. However, branded franchises linked to established corporate chains with additional services may boast general better business credentials demonstrating company oversight and training protocols. Since care spans only hours, most states mandate centers strictly follow childcare licensing procedures around background checks, facility cleanliness, safety precautions, teacher credentials, and legal liability. Scrutinize these minimums first without assumptions.

Pros and Cons of Each Childcare Type

Numerous childcare options exist meeting family needs, budgets and schedules. When selecting programming, consider advantages and disadvantages of each format weighing priorities. Assess your values scheduling adequate time researching referrals knowing no one-size-fits-all.

Daycare Centers
Pros

- Structured curriculum and activities
- Indoor/outdoor facilities
- State licensing and oversight
- Parental smartphone apps tracking kids
- Develops social skills with peers
- Additional services like sports, languages, summer camps
- Qualified teachers often with specialties
- NAEYC accreditation available

Cons

- High teacher turnover from burnout
- Germ exposures with large groups
- Long waitlists and difficulty getting spots
- Less flexible hourly commitments
- High costs - average over $900 monthly
- Closures on major holidays

Preschool Programs
Pros

- Learning foundations for kindergarten preparation
- Small class sizes and cozy environments
- Arts infusions nurturing creativity
- Field trips and guests enhancing themes
- Parent-teacher partner communication
- School district alignments

Cons

- Part-time hours often just Monday-Thursday
- Limited ages served - mainly 3-5 years old
- Waitlists for placement into best options
- No transportation provided
- Teacher burnout and turnover over time
- Tuition can exceed $1000+ monthly

In-Home Daycares
Pros
- Small groups with mixed ages
- Home setting feeling less institutional
- Outdoor play areas at residences
- Overnight/weekend/flexible care sometimes
- Lower costs - often under $800 per month
- Family-style bonding between providers and kids

Cons
- Variable state regulation and oversight
- Risk of abuse and lack of witnesses
- Staffing gaps if provider gets sick
- Limited physical indoor space
- Care duration capped if providers burn out
- Slow removal and discipline policies

Nanny Care
Pros
- Personalized one-on-one attention
- Flexible hours aligned to family needs
- Consistent caregivers long-term
- Cultural or bilingual immersion options
- Overnight and travel care continuity
- Enhanced safety staying home versus commuting elsewhere

Cons
- Isolation from peer social interactions
- Heavy screen time supervision gaps
- Lack of skills generalization across settings
- Difficult affordability unless quite wealthy

- Harsh termination unlikely holding household jobs
- Tax/labor legalities handling household staff

Babysitting Co-ops
Pros

- Extremely low cost trades saving money
- Consistent caregiver options gotten to know well
- Neighborhood networking and friendship-building
- Gear/clothing sharing across ages in group
- Stable rotations and availability
- Ideal for part-time or vacation needs

Cons

- Administering equitable exchange tracking
- Unqualified supervision by non-teachers (parents)
- Home safety risks and liability uncertainty
- Failures if members flake needing back-up plans still
- Poor long-term consistency as kids age
- Weak ongoing developmental enrichment focus

Overnight Care
Pros

- Addresses round-the-clock need gaps
- Continuous care when family unavailable
- Meets needs outside regular business hours
- Special support handling unique family situations
- Provides kids' security and stability
- Trusted alternative from risky ad-hoc babysitters

Cons

- Interrupts child's sleep rhythms and home life
- Difficult facilitating learning while kids tired
- Scarce accommodating kids with special needs or disabilities

- Rare - limited regional availability
- State regulations remain under-developed
- Expensive overnight staffing 24/7

Special Needs Care
Pros

- Licensed therapists reinforce development
- Adaptive technologies and mobility equipment
- Customized curriculum and communication systems fit unique needs
- Higher caregiver-to-child ratios
- Inclusion assistance mainstreaming children
- Parent networking and advocacy empowerment

Cons

- Requires formal medical diagnoses
- Part-time hours may not meet full needs
- Costly specialized facility accommodations
- Paperwork and funding barriers delay access
- Fewer facilities and extended waitlists
- Psychologically taxing for staff over time

Drop-In Care
Pros

- Affordable hourly rates without contracts
- Convenient locations to run errands nearby
- Immediate reservations including last minute
- Flexible blocks of time from 1-4 hrs as needed
- Alleviates scrambling for emergency care
- Provides kids fun outlet from usual routine

Cons

- Upper limits allow only several hours maximum
- No reliable long-term care solution
- High teacher turnover and sparse training

- Weak educational enrichment curriculums
- Changing cast of classroom peers
- Health risks from shared tight facilities

Evaluating these childcare variables helps streamline the best arrangements suiting family logistics, learning priorities, medical needs and household budgets maximizing work-life balance.

CHAPTER 2

MARKET RESEARCH

Conducting thorough market research is crucial for assessing parent needs/preferences in your area and gauging the competition. This section offers techniques and resources to analyze demand factors such as demographics, existing provider rates/ differentiators and barriers that your unique center offering could help alleviate.

Researching Childcare Needs in Your Area

Performing market research lays pivotal groundwork before launching a childcare business determining real community needs, ideal locations, competitive landscape, and projected enrollment rates guiding operational decisions. Collect both statistics and anecdotal data surveying families around targeted service areas.

Child Population Statistics

Analyze census data tracking numbers of children below age 6 residing within a defined geographic radius comprising your prospective customer base. Seek site locations where ample birthrates sustain ongoing regional demand as babies mature through private school eligibility.

Metropolitan statistical areas detail population breakdowns by age brackets and zip codes identifying high-density family zones. Rural towns may rely on state city data cross-referencing school district size estimating overall childhood subsets.

Approximate how many potential clients live around prospective spots also factoring residential growth patterns and community development forecasts likely yielding forthcoming referrals over time beyond current enrollments. Compare multiple sites weighing sufficient concentrations to support present and forthcoming ventures.

Parent Surveys

Once identifying data-driven target areas with adequate child inhabitants, directly survey parents within those sectors about unmet supervision needs. Create online polls or paper questionnaires asking:

- What type(s) of care do you currently utilize?
- What ages of your kids require care?
- What hours/days do you need coverage for work?
- If you miss work when kids are sick or daycare closes?
- Your preferred teacher-to-child ratio range?
- Average monthly budget for care expenses?
- Which amenities most influence selections?
- What dissatisfies you about current arrangements?

Leave open comment sections welcoming personalized experiences or suggestions building community rapport. Provide email signups if willing to share future updates about groundbreaking progress. Analyze results calculating viable participation rates from those compelled to sign up for launch announcements despite no current solution participation. Convert interested leads into project ambassadors.

Local Data Mining

Search online databases aggregating regional statistics about area family dynamics including:

- School district performance reports tracking enrollment fluctuations
- Economic development authority infographics about population gains/losses
- Public health records on incubator discharge rates
- City planning department occupancy permitting for erected daycares
- Nonprofit community needs assessments regarding child services

Compare historical transactions quantifying demand momentum from both public and proprietary sources blended together. Purchase third-party proprietary analyses by respected research firms if budget allows maximizing visibility into granular trends.

Community Leader Interviews

Schedule exploratory meetings with influential leaders. Interact often with young families. Ask pediatricians, school principals, PTA presidents, moms club chairs, recreational directors, library programmers, nonprofit directors etc. what recurrent childcare barriers or frustrations they hear parents facing routinely.

Inquire if any glaring mismatches exist between family expectations and local offerings like schedule conflicts or demographic access gaps. Record candid outside opinions from those experiencing secondary effects if subpar care options. Verify assumptions welcoming constructive criticism before dedicating extensive financial resources. Develop solutions addressing genuine complaints.

Parent Intercept Events

Host community focus groups or information sessions targeted towards family demographics most aligned with projected program offerings. For example, set up booths at kindergarten enrollment fairs, school open house nights or library toddler activity hours. Stop interested passersby for quick dot polling about ideal care characteristics or gauging potential enrollment rates.

Capture contact info by raffling free childcare swag bags to spark viral word-of-mouth referrals. Leverage existing community forums interfacing directly with key parent circles rather than reinventing outreach channels from scratch. Piggyback where target segments already congregate.

Analyze Gaps & Refine Plan

Glean operational insights from research patterns identifying family frustrations. Find teaching philosophies, schedules or specialty offerings missing locally addressing unmet needs. Refine business plans responding to genuine community voiced hardships around care access, flexibility, diversity or affordability. Carve out mission-driven services aligned to fix regional deficiencies delighting families. Let real problematic symptoms highlight guide solutions rendered rather than assumptions or anecdotes. Base every new center facet on local area dialogs and data dispatching targeted help families request directly.

Identifying Your Target Market

Defining an ideal target market and niche aligns marketing directly with compatible families while streamlining enrollment and programming towards specialized offerings matching distinct needs. Clarify which customer segment your model best suits through market research.

Demographic Factors

Segment potential families based on key characteristics like:

Household Incomes: Higher earners afford premium tuition rates while lower-middle income groups need budget conscious options and income-based assistance.

Children's Ages: Center layouts accommodate physical abilities from infant rooms up through school-age recreation. Those serving only certain brackets focus design and lessons suitable for those skills.

Special Needs: Centers inclusive of disabilities require adaptive technologies, specialized therapists and modified teacher-to-student ratios. Mainstream-only sites refer out for additional supports.

Medical Factors: Children facing health conditions like severe allergies or tube feedings require customized meal plans and nursing care integrating treatment regimens into daily programming.

Family Structures: Single, married and separated parents need varying drop-off/pick-up flexibility, joint custody accommodations and affordable scaling for multi-child discounts to cover sole breadwinner scenarios.

Values: Progressive, religious, cultural, creative, academic and ethical approaches appeal uniquely across diverse families prioritizing varied enrichment exposures.

Location: Urban, suburban and rural geographies determine if parents commute to centralized centers or need accessible neighborhood establishments within residential communities.

Parental Work Factors

Parent work schedules directly influence child supervision needs regarding:

Commuting Distances: Those working locally utilize more convenient, proximate options while commuters can drop-off along highways en-route if centers locate strategically along employment corridors.

Weekly Schedules: Standard daytime, second shift, night shift, weekend and rotating schedules require coinciding programming with consistent oversight until parents return home.

Overtime Unpredictability: Salaried professionals working late sporadically need forgiving pick-up policies or late fees compared to hourly workers punching timecards.

Job Flexibility: Strict hourly workers desire reliable center hours while self-employed parents handle more variability dropping off kids unpredictably.

High-Pressure Careers: Intense jobs like medicine prohibit disruptions when emergencies happen so late pick-ups cannot jeopardize employment. More lenient professions allow occasional scheduling hiccups.

Job Transfers: Military, deportation services, missionary and State Department families move often requiring consistency welcoming new enrollments mid-year despite disruptions.

Start-Up Type Influences

Finally, business models hinge on:

Profit Status: Nonprofits subsidize tuition for disadvantaged groups often underserved with few local options while for-profit centers must fundraise to make payroll and keep doors open.

Business Sponsorship: Church funded programs support member families while corporately sponsored centers serve working parents aligned to headquarters. Universities teach future educators while also caring for kids. Government initiatives target military families or workforce development.

Program Intervention Model: Low-income programs incentivize family goal setting while special needs interventions coordinate extensive therapies and mainstreaming help. Standardized curriculum prepares upper-middle class kids for academic success.

Social Change Mission: Outreach providing harder-to-serve groups education justice expands societal equity. Which families most need better access or opportunity in your region?

Customizing operations explicitly towards a defined target market reduces diffusion meeting too many needs missing the mark for any particular subset. Narrow specialization makes enrollment, lesson planning, budgeting and marketing more efficient excelling for niche demographics.

Learning Licensing and Regulations

All childcare facilities must comply with state licensing and regulations to legally operate protecting children's health, safety and wellbeing. Requirements govern teacher credentials, health precautions, safety protocols, nutrition, facilities, emergency procedures and curriculum.

State Licensing

Child Care licensing establishes baseline standards for consistent quality avoiding dangers from unmonitored providers. Parents can file complaints about regulatory violations to state agencies managing oversight through unannounced annual inspections assessing:

Staff Backgrounds: Teachers must pass criminal history checks without records of violent crimes, sex offenses or child abuse/neglect charges. Also need current pediatric CPR/first aid certification, early childhood staff trainings and proper skill credentials. Directors require administrative credentials and experience.

Health Precautions: Staff continually monitor children's illnesses quarantining obviously sick kids. Policies detail symptom-free periods before rejoining groups after infections along with hand hygiene essentials diminishing contagions. Cleaning protocols meet sanitation requirements.

Physical Safety: Facilities must pass fire inspections with functional detectors, extinguishers and posted evacuation procedures. Security systems control entry access. Hazardous materials stay locked away while childproofing eliminates dangers. Toys meet safety standards for each age bracket by size. Outdoor playgrounds need protective surfacing. Staff actively supervise activities to prevent injury risks.

Caregiver Responsiveness: Warm nurturing caregiver relationships ensure trust and attachment security monitoring emotional needs and signs of abuse at home. Open communication channels welcome parent partnership in child development plans responding to emerging needs.

Nutrition: Meal components meet healthy USDA-aligned childhood nutrition guidelines including portion sizes scaled appropriately to ages served. Snacks and meals follow timed schedules posted publicly accounting for dietary restrictions like allergies. Staff trained in safe food prep and infant bottle handling reinforcing healthy relationships around eating.

Facilities: Entry access protocols prevent child abduction ensuring only approved parental pickups. Interior spaces labeled clearly designating functions and age appropriateness. Ventilation, plumbing, regulations around diapering stations, cots, cribs and developmental learning spaces reinforce safety cleanliness. Required posting publicly display licensing credentials demonstrating current compliance status without deficiencies.

Education Approach: Curriculum standards nurture social, physical, emotional and cognitive growth through group/individual activities respecting abilities at each age. Routines balance both nurturing care and kindergarten preparation across infants through early school years.

Infractions yield citations compelling prompt corrections with potential shutdowns or probation for consistent violations over time after opportunity for remediation. Unlicensed operations wither fast under fines so full adherence remains imperative.

Local Regulations

Beyond statewide licensing policy, also verify additional municipal rules like zoning restrictions on commercial businesses residential districts, square footage requirements per child, parking allowances reducing neighborhood disruption, pick-up/drop off queue limitations and outdoor playtime noise curfews. City planning departments detail allowable usage specifications in submissions for occupancy permitting and running home businesses.

Liability insurance brokers also explain extra riders needed conducting operations involving high-risk children on premises including umbrella protections capping payouts from incidents. Insurance covers both medical and legal expenses defending accident claims unless negligence proved. Some cities mandate insurance minimums as a prerequisite to issue business licenses allowing new centers opening doors to the public.

Pre-operational consultations with municipal agencies ensure full legal compliance for all local statutes before welcoming precious young families trusting care and education to unfamiliar new owners. Rules exist protecting limited family resources from financial or emotional hardship if providers underperform.

Accreditation Standards

Voluntary accreditation through the National Association for the Education of Young Children (NAEYC) demonstrates commitment to exceeding baseline state licensing through 300+ elevated standards continuously improving program quality, curriculum offerings, community outreach, ethical leadership, teacher support and family partnerships guided by child development research. NAEYC rigorously evaluates both structural fairness and process consistency, awarding 10 year terms of excellence after extensive review. High performers distinguish centers possessing developmentally appropriate learning environments benefitting young minds. Nearly 20% of American early childhood centers currently obtain NAEYC marks showcasing optimal outcomes improving lives.

Understanding the Competition

Analyzing competitive forces clarifies market positioning for new childcare businesses distinguishing offerings providing unique value able to coexist locally among prevailing players. Track direct rivals, identify unmet niches through parent surveys and size-up barriers impeding entry or sustainability long-run.

Inventory Direct Competitors

Drive around geographical target zones documenting all current child care establishments' visibility firsthand. Note site locations, advertised ages/operating hours served, facility square footage sizes, outdoor play structures and posted tuition rates listed.

Search small business databases confirming licensed providers on record around areas of interest cross-referencing on-the-ground findings. State licensing agencies list compliant facilities passing annual health inspections.

Search crowdsource review platforms like Yelp to check parent ratings and recommendations of incumbent establishments learn reputations. Identify both well-rated favorites likely patronized steadily plus any lower scored locations signaling potential business vulnerabilities unable to satisfy families adequately.

Segment Competitors

Classify regional centers by service models offered from the options below to understand variety available vying for local market share:

- **Standard Daycare**: Open weekday business hours for regular needs
- **Specialty Education:** Specific cultural immersion or academic focal points
- **Corporate On-Site:** Employer subsidized childcare for adjacent workers
- **Before/After School Care:** Aligning only with K-12 academic calendars/hours
- **Preschool Only:** Part-day developmental early learning programs

- **Special Needs Intervention:** Facilities and therapies adapted for disabilities
- **In-Home Family Childcare:** Neighborhood nanny services run from private residences
- **Seasonal Care:** Summertime or school holiday supervision options

Some competitors integrate across multiple segments. But categorizing business models maps coverage gaps signaling potential customer groups underserved currently within the region.

Parent Survey Input

Directly collect consumer feedback around regional childcare pain points through online surveys or impromptu focus groups. Ask:

- What options parents currently choose and why?
- What aspects families enjoy about current arrangements?
- What key frustrations or limitations exist driving any dissatisfaction?
- Would improved locations, hours, program focal areas, group sizes, or budgetary control retain more enrollment loyalty over time?
- How likely are prospects to recommend current providers friends/colleagues?

Isolate actionable input illuminating specific unresolved complaints justifying competitors' churn beyond typical switch rotations normal from kids aging up across school transitions anyway regardless. Identify recurring themes where new entrants could delight through policies improving upon status quo options.

SWOT Analysis

Finally, consolidate research benchmarking current industry players' inherent:

Strengths: Successful elements securing strong market footholds based on crowdsource ratings and community reputations

Weaknesses: Flaws or service gaps contributing to lukewarm feedback where users desire better experiences

Opportunities: Project growth trajectories building on existing platform strengths as regional demographics expand

Threats: External risks jeopardizing durability if unable to adapt against demographic shifts, cultural expectations or competitive substitutions

These insights brainstorm strategic differentiation making newcomer offerings standout. Where competitors falter, craft benefits aligned better to parent wish lists and kid enjoyment leveraging analytics honing competitive advantages. Track industry innovations adjusting service models to satisfy modern families continually. Identify new technologies like apps improving convenience engagement parents prioritize in daily decisions determining loyalty beyond just physical utilities.

Setting Competitive Prices

When starting a childcare business, one of the most important considerations is determining what to charge families for your services. Setting the right prices is crucial for covering your operating costs and turning a profit. In this section, we'll explore competitive pricing and the factors to consider when setting your rates.

Research Local Childcare Rates

The first step is researching what other local childcares charge. Get quotes from at least 5 other centers and in-home daycares in your area. Take note of their:

- Hourly, daily and weekly rates
- Discounts for multi-child families
- Registration/supply fees
- Payment policies

This market research will give you an idea of the going rates in your region. Don't copy the prices exactly — you'll want to find ways to differentiate. But this information helps you set competitive pricing.

Calculate Your Costs

Next, dig into your own expenses. Tally up fixed costs like:

- Rent
- Utilities
- Insurance
- Furnishings
- Technology

And variable costs per child like:

- Staff wages & benefits
- Food & supplies
- Educational materials
- Enrichment activities

Based on enrollments, determine your total monthly costs. Then divide by the number of children to find your **break-even point** — the bare minimum you need to charge.

Set Target Profit Margins

Don't just aim to break even. A healthy profit margin of 10-20%+ ensures sustainability. Compute:

(Break-Even + Target Profit) x Number of Children = Total Revenue Needed

Divide revenue needed by max capacity for your **base daily rate per child**. Add premiums for infants, extra hours, etc. Review against competitor rates and adjust.

Consider Discounts & Incentives

Offer sibling, military, teacher or multi-day discounts to attract families:

- 10% off second sibling
- 15% off third+ sibling
- 10-15% first responder discount

- 5-7% discount for 5+ day signups

First month free deals, referral rewards, loyalty programs — anything driving volume helps offset costs.

Update Pricing Over Time

Re-evaluate pricing 6-12 months after launch. Compute actual fixed & variable costs. If you overestimated expenses initially, pass some savings to families. If operating costs grew, small boosts to rates may be needed. Updating as needed keeps you competitive.

Competitive yet affordable pricing is challenging, but optimizing rates for your operating model and market is key to succeeding as a childcare business. Analyze costs diligently, maximize enrollments — and update based on real-life data. This keeps your finances healthy while serving families.

CHAPTER 3

BUSINESS PLANS

Elements of a Crafting a viable business plan represents a foundational step when launching any childcare organization--communicating your strategy and financial forecasts to gain initial investor support. This chapter explains each section and projections within typical childcare business plans.

Business Plan

Crafting a strong business plan is essential for anyone looking to open a childcare center. This strategic document covers everything from your business concept to financial projections, serving as both a roadmap for opening and guide for operating. In this section, we'll break down the core elements to include in your plan.

Executive Summary

Briefly summarize your business goals and proposition. Explain the major details covered throughout the full plan. This section hooks readers and gets them oriented. Key details to include:

- Business concept/offerings
- Target market & location details
- Competitive advantages
- Management team & staff overview

- Financial outlook & capital requirements
- Expected growth trajectory & projections

Keep it to 1-2 pages maximizing impact. Consider writing this last after nailing down all details.

Company Overview

Provide an in-depth look at your management team and operational plan. Cover details like:

- Ownership structure & key staff members
- Licenses, credentials & certifications held
- Services offered, enrollment capacity & classroom arrangements
- Locations details, square footage & facility highlights
- Hours of operation, typical schedules & curriculum methods
- Safety & security protocols and features

This gives readers a feel for how your center will run day-to-day.

Market Analysis

Demonstrate a strong grasp of your target childcare market. Analyze details like:

- Area demographics, including number of families with young children
- Local economic outlook & trends supporting services
- Competitors in the region, their offerings & current rates
- Gaps/weaknesses amongst existing options you can capitalize on
- Volume of prospective customers in the zone you can attract

Proving demand and strategic positioning against other options builds confidence.

Financial Plan & Projections

Show a viable path to profitability over time. Break out expected:

- Startup costs — permits, renovations, supplies
- Operating expenses — rent, payroll, supplies, etc.
- Enrollment targets & revenue projections
- Capital/financing needs & intended sources

Model profit & loss, balance sheet and cash flows across the first 5 years. This demonstrates sustainability.

With solid planning around these core elements — your offerings, team, market dynamics, and finances — you set your childcare business up for success in both opening and ongoing operations. Use your plan to sell your vision to funders, employees and families too.

Financial Projections

Creating detailed financial projections is vital for assessing the viability of your childcare business and securing funding. By modeling expected costs, revenues and other key financial metrics over the first 5 years, you can determine if your concept pencils out. This section will cover building essential projections.

Startup Costs

Calculate an itemized list of expected one-time startup expenses, like:

- Market research
- Business incorporation fees
- Rent deposits
- Renovations & facility setup
- Furnishings, toys & educational materials
- Licensing & permits
- Starting inventory
- Website development

- Marketing activities
- Contingency buffer

Tally it all for your **total startup costs**. This informs funding needs.

Operating Costs

Estimate ongoing monthly operating expenses, including:

- Rent & utilities
- Facility maintenance & cleaning
- Office supplies & printing
- Food, diapers & other consumable supplies
- Licensing, insurance & other fixed costs
- Payroll, payroll taxes & employee benefits
- Accounting & legal fees
- Advertising
- Credit card processing fees

Define expenses annually accounting for inflation.

Revenue Forecasts

Project your **total revenue** based on:

- Size of facility & target max enrollment by age
- Ages served & ratio of infants vs. toddlers vs. preschoolers
- Daily, weekly and monthly rates to be charged
- Expected percentage occupancy over time

Conservatively grow enrollment, occupancy and rates.

Profit & Loss Statement

Subtract your operating expenses from revenue forecasts to model your net profit. Add estimated:

- One-time startup costs
- Tax rates
- Depreciation

Account for profit drivers like economies of scale over time.

Review, refine and finalize accurate monthly projections showing profitability within 12-24 months. Now you have compelling financials to share in your business plan for sourcing capital and convincing staff & families the care center will thrive. Continuously revisit projections against actual performance.

Sources of Funding and Financing Options

Launching a childcare business requires significant upfront capital. From covering startup costs to maintaining smooth cash flow as enrollment builds, you need financial runway. This section explores funding and financing options entrepreneurs can consider, including:

Personal Savings

The number one source of capital for most small businesses is the owner's personal savings. Tapping into money you have socked away provides flexibility and autonomy. Evaluate your current cash reserves and determine an amount you feel comfortable investing into the launch. Any savings helps reduce the amount needing external financing.

Friends & Family Investors

Bootstrapping from friends and family who believe in your abilities is another popular funding avenue. Offer investment shares tied to your ownership stake. Draw up promissory agreements outlining repayment terms like:

- Repaid in 36 months
- 7% APR interest
- $X upfront investment
- Y% equity share

Set clear expectations upfront around timelines and their role, if any, in operations.

Business Loans & Lines of Credit

Financial institutions can provide startup funding or revolving credit to tap when expenses exceed revenues during slower months. Compare loan and line amounts, rates, terms, collateral requirements and qualifications among banks and credit unions to determine the best fit option.

Government Programs

Explore Small Business Administration resources like microloans and Women/Minority-owned grants. Non-profit microfinance groups are another option providing low interest loans. Qualify for childcare specific funding programs available locally and federally.

Crowdfunding

Launch a campaign through a site like Kickstarter or Indiegogo. Describe your business goals creatively through a video and campaign page regulators and parents can share. Offer rewards for contributions like free months of care, branded merchandise or naming classrooms. Set a funding minimum and deadline.

Evaluate the type timing, cost and terms of funding against current and future cash flow projections. When derived from personal assets, payback periods can be more flexible. Debt instruments shift risk but add financing expenses so model repayment carefully. Fund operations conservatively, pursing options allowing you to maintain control.

Choosing a Business Structure

When starting a childcare business, one of the first legal decisions you'll make is choosing an ownership structure. Consult with an attorney and accountant to determine which set-up suits your goals and operational plans best. Weigh options like:

Sole Proprietorship

This simple structure means you alone own the business, personally responsible for liabilities. Low start-up costs and complete managerial control comes with risk through unlimited liability. Sole proprietors report profits & losses on personal tax returns. If looking to operate a small in-home daycare, this presents a decent option needing less formal registration.

Partnership

In this structure, ownership responsibilities are shared between two or more individuals who want to manage the business together. A formal partnership agreement outlining equity splits, decision making authority, responsibilities, etc. is strongly advised. Partners jointly share in any profits and debts allowing for shared risk and investment. Different arrangements on control and liability can be defined.

Limited Liability Company (LLC)

LLCs shield your personal assets like savings accounts and real estate from business-related liabilities, only risking the business's assets instead. LLC's provide liability protections like a corporation with the pass-through tax benefits of a partnership or sole proprietorship avoiding double taxation. Members can customize management and profit distributions through agreement. Setup and operating costs are reasonably affordable. This presents the best of both worlds for many small business owners seeking those twin benefits.

S Corporation

Like LLC's, S corporations avoid double taxation — owners pay taxes on profits & losses only once personally, not at both corporate and shareholder levels. There are limitations however, like only allowing one class of stock and up to 100 shareholders; requiring directors and shareholder meetings; and more complex record keeping and reporting requirements. State registration and compliance costs are also typically higher for Corporations.

Think about your goals for personal liability protection, raising capital, accounting preferences, and shareholder agreements when selecting the right structure. Weigh control, governance complexity and tax implications. Childcare centers make smart choices going the LLC or S-Corp route. Consult accounting and legal guidance to evaluate your best option.

Tax Implications

The legal structure you choose for your childcare business impacts how you will be taxed—so understanding key implications is important. Consult an accountant to map out the best strategy based on entity choice, income sources, deductions opportunities, filing requirements, and more. We'll overview central considerations.

Business Structures

Sole proprietors report profits/losses, make quarterly estimated payments, and file schedules with personal returns. Partners file informational partnership returns allocating profit/loss to partners. LLCs and S corps similarly pass gains/losses to owners who pay taxes. C corporations report income and shareholders pay dividends/capital gains tax. Your structure drives forms filed and income reporting.

Income Taxes

If setup as a sole proprietorship, partnership, LLC, or S corp, the IRS does not directly tax business income. Rather it passes to your personal return. You will owe annual income taxes on net earnings at your personal rate—which varies based on level. C Corps pay corporate income taxes (21%) separately from dividends owners receive.

Self-Employment Taxes

Sole proprietors must pay 15.3% self-employment (SE) taxes on net income to fund Social Security and Medicare (halved after exceeding income thresholds). General partners also owe SE taxes; Limited partners may on guaranteed payments. LLC members can elect to be taxed as partners, so responsible for SE taxes, or corporate directors exempt from SE taxes.

Employer Taxes

Any employees you hire require you to pay state and federal employer taxes like Medicare, unemployment insurance, and social security from gross wages. Ensure you account for the full ~15% payroll tax burden when budgeting staff expenses.

Sales Taxes

Daycare services may be exempt from sales tax depending on state laws. However, you likely need to collect and remit sales taxes on taxable goods sold or fees for extra offerings that qualify based on local jurisdictions.

Consider estimated quarterly payments on income to avoid underpayment penalties. Keep immaculate records capturing allowable deductions too. Accountants help navigate business tax intricacies.

CHAPTER 4

LICENSING AND REGULATIONS

Navigating federal, state and local licensing regulations requires due diligence to open legally, maintain ongoing compliance and ensure safety. Review common rules around age groups, facilities, staffing, nutrition and curriculum that owners must satisfy.

Learning State and Local Licensing Regulations

Every state establishes its own set of standards and licensing protocols that childcare centers must comply with to operate legally. Regulations focus on protecting children's health, safety and wellbeing but vary across jurisdictions when it comes to specifics. In this section, we'll break down key licensing essentials.

Researching Requirements

First, thoroughly research all regulations in your state for the type of care you aim to provide. Extensive materials outlining codes and statutes, application processes and fees, reporting rules, allowed ages and capacities, staff qualifications, health precautions, nutrition, disciplinary policies, built environment mandates and more will be available from your:

- State Health and Human Services Department

- Department of Early Education and Care
- Child Care Resource and Referral Agency

Additionally, contact your city or county government for local municipal rules on zoning, building construction/renovations and fire safety restricting locations and facility set up for childcares. Mastering the full gamut ensures compliance.

Minimum Standards

While particulars differ, common baseline requirements exist like:

- Child to staff ratios — i.e. 4:1 for infants, 10:1 preschoolers
- Group sizes — age segmented class pods
- Caregiver age, background check, experience and training requirements
- Annual licenses and mid-year inspections
- Records retention — emergency contacts, attendance, health reports
- Developmentally appropriate learning standards and activities
- Medication dispensing protocols
- Nutrition and meal standards

These serve to protect safety and align with early childhood development best practices.

State websites let you browse the rules in detail or allow childcare owners in planning to directly reach out to licensing agents with questions during the preparatory process. Establish written policies and procedures reflecting regulations to train staff to uphold standards keyed to renewal.

Successfully accomplishing licensure demonstrates to parents your services meet quality markers, an advantage over informal options lacking oversight. So while the process involves effort, regulations ultimately safeguard the children in your care and community trust in your brand.

Zoning Restrictions

Local zoning ordinances dictate locations within a city or town where childcare businesses can operate. Understanding these land use restrictions during site selection prevents headaches. Zoning aims to create logical, safe separations between residential areas and commercial activities within jurisdictions. Childcares traditionally fall under civic, educational or commercial use designations. We'll review typical zoning factors and requirements you'll need to investigate when planning locations.

Residential Districts

Some suburban or rural neighborhoods with limited commercial zones do allow childcare centers to open within residential areas under certain home occupation conditional use exemptions. These usually limit signage, staff count, hours, visible exterior modifications and number of children served. On-site outdoor play space meeting square footage minimums per child enrolled will need preserving too.

Urban residential zoning more commonly restricts commercial enterprise mixing limiting feasibility without a use variance hearing. Noise, traffic and parking pressures make approval difficult unless few other childcare options exist nearby.

Educational & Institutional Districts

Siting centers within designated educational zones— common for preschool based programs or those leasing unused school capacity—eliminates zoning roadblocks. Houses of worship similarly make compatible institutional co-location partners under exempted religious assembly allowed uses.

Commercial Districts

Commercial areas like shopping centers, plazas or

standalone buildings along busy roads generally allow childcares, especially within mixed-use developments. However, proximity to bars, cannabis dispensaries or adult entertainment often gets barred. If focused on commercial properties, confirm:

- CC or CD zoning classifications permit educational facilities
- No buffer distance requirements apply limiting proximity to other establishments that could risk safety

Critical Steps

First verify candidate sites' designated zoning and if childcare constitutes an approved use. Being incorrectly classified or violating separation buffers risks shutdown and code enforcement fines. Some zones require special exceptions or conditional use permits too, needing approvals before operating.

Finally, check for sufficient parking availability, accessible entryways meeting ADA laws, compliant fire exits, necessary ventilation, and other structural mandates childcares must provide. Only lease/purchase locations where legal location qualifications get satisfied.

Immunization, Training and Background Check Requirements

To protect children's health and safety, states mandate childcare workers meet certain requirements including: obtaining immunizations, completing regular training, and passing background checks. Parents trust providers comply. We'll outline common staff qualification rules.

Staff Immunizations

Requiring current vaccinations for infectious diseases like measles, whooping cough, and the flu limits contagion risks. Common daycare staffer mandates include:

- Annual flu vaccine

- Tdap booster every 10 years
- 1-2 MMR vaccines
- Hepatitis A and/or B series

Some states allow exemptions with physician letters when the person's health contraindicates a vaccine. Others mandate termination for noncompliance given public health priorities. Know your regional policies.

For highly infectious illnesses like chickenpox, required minimum exclusion periods from work exist too after exposure. Follow protocols like masking, sanitization, and notifications to parents of incidents and immunity guidance.

Background Checks

Nearly all states require licensing background checks on directors, employees and any volunteers having unsupervised access to children. Typical requirements delve into:

- Criminal history — convictions or pending cases
- Sex offender registries
- Child abuse and neglect determinations

Individuals with disqualifying records are barred from childcare employment. Some states enumerate specific barrier crimes while others provide discretion on evaluating findings. Expect fingerprints and/or FBI record submissions meeting nationwide, multi-state standards too. Checks renew every 2-5 years.

Early Childhood Training Requirements

Annual ongoing education ensures teachers implement appropriate curriculums, behavioral modification techniques, health protocols and developmental milestones guidance.

Infant caregivers may need related credentials or CPR certification. Some states specify hourly requirements by role like 12 hours annually for administrators, 20 for lead preschool teachers plus blood-borne pathogen courses.

Maintain dated staff transcripts and skills profiles proving policy adherence. Training generates better teacher retention outcomes too while keeping safety and care quality high.

Complying with health, safety and competency qualification mandates takes diligence but pays off protecting kids, limiting risks and positioning your center as an premium option committed to excellence. Make funding professional growth standard and stay abreast of updated state regulations. The effort bolsters community trust in your brand.

Safety, Security and Health Codes

Given the constant activity and high energy of small kids, creating a properly controlled care setting meeting rigorous safety and health benchmarks takes forethought and investment. We'll review regulations and best practices owners must implement to earn licensing, parent trust and positive program outcomes.

Staff-to-Child Ratios

Assigning adequate supervised staff for the number of children in attendance prevents accidents and injuries while enabling learning. Common required ratios by age include:

- 1 teacher per 3-4 infants
- 1 teacher per 4-6 toddlers
- 1 teacher per 8-10 preschoolers
- 1 teacher per 10-12 school age children

Group sizes stay limited too—like to 12 infants, 18 preschoolers max. When open, at least two adults must be present in case of emergencies. Program directors themselves cannot count toward ratios, requiring separate coverage.

Physical Space Requirements

Centers need commercial-grade, compliant facilities accommodating young bodies. Infants remain restricted to safe floor play given climbing and mobility limits. All children require ample indoor activity space—typically 35+ square feet room to play per child depending on licensure minimums.

Outdoor playgrounds serve essential too but with certified age-appropriate equipment like soft padded ground surfaces under climbing sets, wood chip ground cover to cushion falls, and guardrails to avoid tumbles. Regular independent inspections verify continued safety. Centers detail security protocols controlling unauthorized access as well. State evaluators ensure the environment suitably protects and enables kids during reviews.

Health & Hygiene Policies

Documented health procedures maintain clean, sanitary facilities resistant to spread of illness. Require kids get physician-OKs before returning post-sickness and monitor for symptoms vigilantly. Follow safe food prep handling course training, diapering protocols separating from eating areas, daily cleanings, toy deep sanitization cycles and handwashing routines. Stock first aid kids, document accidents, and log medications centrally. Regular lice checks support prevention too. Sharp attention to policies keeps sickness transmission risks in check.

Meeting higher care benchmarks distinguishes your offering while letting kids play, grow and explore freely within guarded settings.

Insurance Requirements

Operating a childcare facility comes with substantial risks given young accident-prone populations interacting daily. State licensing boards thus mandate centers carry adequate insurance policies to mitigate legal and financial liabilities if safety incidents occur. Review regional requirements and consult brokers to secure necessary coverages.

Commercial General Liability

This protects from costly third party property damage, bodily injuries, personal injuries and advertising offense claims. It covers both legal defense fees and judgements up to policy limits. Care centers need at least $1 million per occurrence and $3 million aggregate with childcare riders given elevated risks. Product and completed operations coverage lasts beyond policy terms also shielding from future claims after opening if issues emerge.

Professional Liability Insurance

Also termed errors and omissions insurance, this covers negligence claims if staff actions cause harm—like not properly watching and securing children leading to an escape or accident. It includes legal defense costs and damages (often $1-5 million limits). Some states mandate E&O policies, especially for larger centers.

Directors & Officers Insurance

If structured as a corporation, directors and officers (D&O) policies defend and cover judgements where board members or executive directors face allegations of wrongful acts. Standard policies often exclude child abuse but enhanced childhood sexual abuse coverage closes this gap.

Workers Compensation

All businesses with staff must carry state-dictated workers compensation protecting employees injured on the job. This covers medical bills, lost wages from missed work, rehabilitation costs and death benefits for families if fatal. Premiums vary based on risk classification, payroll size and injury histories.

Evaluate all commercial policies during licensing and renew insurance continuously operating. Consult brokers specialized in childcare industry risks for proper coverage guarding the business.

CHAPTER 5

STAFF AND OPERATIONS

Recruiting knowledgeable teachers able to nurture growth across infants to school-aged children proves essential for program quality. This section offers best practices for hiring roles, training staff and structuring your center's workflows from security policies to technology use.

Teacher-to-Child Ratios

Staffing your childcare center appropriately with enough teachers and aides to safely supervise the number of children in attendance is imperative for safety and compliance with state laws. Guidelines and requirements vary by group size and child age. Let's analyze common ratios and considerations when planning staff levels.

Ratio Guidelines

The following teacher-to-child ratios set baseline recommendations that providers aim to stay within or outperform:

- Infants (6 weeks to 12 months): 1 caregiver per 3-4 infants
- Toddlers (12 months to 36 months) 1 caregiver per 4-6 toddlers
- Preschoolers (36 months to 5 years): 1 caregiver per

10-12 preschoolers
- School Age (5 years to 12 years): 1 caregiver per 15-20 school age

Ratios tighten for younger ages needing closer care and support hit key developmental milestones. When age groups commingle like during opening/closing transitions, default to the stricter ratio.

Other Factors Influencing Ratios

While age sets helpful benchmarks, individual needs play a role too. The more children exhibiting special needs enrolled requiring specialized attention to thrive alters ratio guidance. Babies also feed, sleep and need diapering on more scattered schedules demanding greater staff availability. Ratios balance safety with costs—the stricter the ratios, the more teachers you need to meet enrollment capacity impacting payroll. As the owner, you cannot count in ratios yourself either—requiring at least two separate staff members always present among groups.

Understanding State Licensing Requirements

Importantly, check your state's legally mandated minimum ratios and group sizes by age which set the compliance floor levels to uphold. While some state ratios mirror recommendations, others diverge—like specifying 1:5 ratios for preschoolers or 1:8 for toddlers as law. Failure to consistently abide by state staffing rules risks fines or license suspensions when injuries arise so knowing precise parameters is key. Some cities or quality assurance programs dictate tighter rules too.

Analyze your target classroom arrangements and ages served. Budget for sufficient teachers and floaters to properly supervise activity recognizing younger ages need extra sets of watchful eyes. While state minimums meet the law, consider boosting ratios where able promoting safety and learning.

Hiring Staff and Teachers

Recruiting warm, passionate and qualified teachers sets the foundation for quality care and learning outcomes. With turnover rates touching 30%, take time finding educators invested in early development able to bolster retention through competitive pay, benefits and training opportunities. Let's review key hiring steps.

Defining Roles

Outline the types of roles and related qualifications needed to deliver your program like:

- Lead Teacher (Infant Room) - Requirements: College degree in early childhood development, 3 years' experience, meets state credentialing
- Assistant Teacher (Toddler Room) - Requirements: High school diploma/GED, 1 year experience, certification preferred
- Floaters - Requirements: High school diploma, basic state training completed
- Cook - Requirements: ServSafe certified, nutrition background

Cover responsibilities and competencies sought given specialized duties with infants or capacities to develop age-tailored lesson plans for older groups. Know state teacher qualification mandates.

Posting Jobs

Market open positions through channels top talent review like industry associations, college career centers and programs feeding early education candidates. Highlight your center's vision, community ties, facility assets and any above-average benefits that set you apart like tuition reimbursement or retirement savings options.

Vetting Applicants

Require submission of full resumes/applications documenting experiences, education, skill sets and state certifications held with a cover letter outlining motivation for the role and connections to young learners. Conduct structured interviews gauging competence, energy, teaching philosophies on childhood development and scenarios testing critical thinking judgement.

Thoroughly checking 2-3 provided references assesses past reliability and care aptitude. Most states mandate fingerprinting and extensive background checks too reviewing for any disqualifying history.

Onboarding & Ongoing Training

Once hired, set clear learning objectives for the first 30/60/90 days. Review center safety protocols, emergency procedures, curriculum standards and family communication policies. Maintain open dialogue fostering comfort raising concerns. Offer subsidized continuing education reimbursing annual training costs upon completion to retain talent. Tap knowledgeable teachers to lead portions of orientation training. Implementing immersive onboarding and ongoing professional development demonstrates the value you place on fostering staff growth while ensuring classrooms run smoothly.

Investing in selective screening, higher wages where possible and progression opportunities pays dividends attracting and retaining superior early childcare educators prepared to thoughtfully serve families.

Staff Management and Retention

With toddler and preschool teacher turnover reaching upwards of 30%, managing staff, boosting morale and strengthening retention is imperative for consistency families depend on. Review proven strategies for supporting and keeping talent long-term.

Competitive Compensation

While tight budgets limit wages, compensating fairly signals value and curbs churn. Explore raising base pay then benchmarking increases to measurable metrics over time like certifications gained, performance levels achieved and years served. Consider end-of-year bonuses too. For less pricey picks, offer commuter cost offsets like gas cards or covered parking. Paid overtime and shift differentials help as well. Even incremental steps through reviews help.

Robust Benefits Options

Look into providing monthly healthcare stipends teachers can use toward independent plans until enrollment scales enough to offer group coverage. Flexible paid time off, sick days and set holidays off preserve sanity. See if 401(k) options apply allowing matching retirement contributions. Reimburse ongoing training investments too. While not all possible initially, phase enhancements in over time.

Avenues for Growth

Create clear designation levels from Assistant Teacher to Lead Teacher to Director mapped to quantifiable skill and competency benchmarks. Outline development opportunities at each rung like tuition reimbursement up to annual limits for those pursuing promotion focused coursework or certifications. Managers coach rising stars on advancement paths. This incentivizes staff to build capacities over many years of commitment to the center community.

Foster Community

Encourage peer mentor relationships between veterans and new hires. Organize occasional group outings and meetups outside work to deepen connections. Show appreciation through small gifts like catered lunches for Teacher Appreciation Week or birthday acknowledgements. Listen closely to feedback shared in stay interviews. People desire fulfilling roles supporting purposeful work and deeper ties.

While not feasible overnight, making thoughtful investments in those caring for children pays dividends through improved classroom continuity benefitting enrolled families.

Curriculums and Activities

Structuring educational programming tailored to each age group's learning abilities promotes cognitive, social-emotional and physical progress. Balancing crafts, play, outdoor time and instruction plays a profound role in early development. Let's review designing curriculums and scheduling days fulfilling all needs.

Infant Care Focus

For infants not yet ambulatory, center on sensory stimulation across sight, sound, touch and motion domains. Develop motor skills through tummy time play, mirror interaction, soft blocks stacking, music and flashing light mobiles stimulating eyes tracking movement. Read simple picture books focusing images supporting recognition. Schedule ample diapering/feeding respectively. Childproof all spaces crawling babies access removing dangers. Plan multiple 30-45 minute naps adjusting to fussy signals. Keep immunization and height/weight trackers current monitoring growth.

Toddler Classrooms

Focus on developing language and socialization through center play rotations, pretend kitchens/shops, sensory tables, coloring stations for fine motor control and picture book reading corners. Introduce basic naming and counting through song games using flash cards and puzzles featuring animals or common objects supporting association and memory capacity development. Allow messy play like non-toxic finger painting and playdough kneading. Provide outdoor trike/scooter/climber equipment under watch teaching coordination supporting mobility independence. Divide into free play, organized activity like crafts and designated snack/meal times on predictable 90-120 minute cycles establishing routine while retaining flexibility responding to energy ebbs/flows.

Preschool Programming

Expand curriculum further reading stories, identifying letters/numbers, naming shapes, categorizing by traits, discussing differences all building symbolic thinking, comprehension and critical analysis abilities. Guide projects introducing scissor usage cutting shapes, weaving laces through punched cardboard, gluing materials when creating art and tracing stencils improving dexterity. Sing songs reinforcing ABC order and 123 sequence through rhythmic repetition. Offer dress-up dramatic play, building block construction, matching games and outdoor organized sports like kickball developing confidence and cooperative teamwork. Leverage field trips — in-house zoo/farm animals visits or community helpers demonstrations make lasting impressions. Academic readiness foundations start now!

Balance this scaffolding across all classrooms tailoring activities and sensory engagement to current, emerging abilities without over programming days. Regularly observe child interactions and milestones achieved to adjust approaches keeping progress on track.

Menus and Snacks

Providing healthy, appealing and balanced snacks and meals ensures children receive needed nutrition supporting growth during long care days. Review key considerations when planning daily menus that sustain energy levels while exposing young palates to varied flavors and food groups.

Meal Guidelines

Consult your state's food and beverage criteria for child daycares standardizing offerings. Common scientifically based standards require fruit/vegetable components be served at every meal. Grains must be whole enriched options. Dairy is included daily—yogurt for toddlers, milk for preschoolers meeting vitamin D and calcium needs aiding bone development. Many mandate low sugar, no added sweeteners rules too avoiding energy spike and crash cycles. Calorie minimums and protein contains apply depending on length of care. Sample 2-week rotating menus then post publicly listing ingredients for parental review ensuring no allergen or sensitivity issues.

Meal Schedule Consistency

Coordinate snack times mid-morning and mid-afternoon to energize kids avoiding hunger based behavioral challenges. Space at least 1.5-2 hours from main lunch service allowing digestion preventing reduced appetite interfering with the primary meal. Providing consistent, timed offerings trains kids' bodies anticipating forthcoming food intake keeping mood even. Post visible picture based clocks or timers so children recognize normal patterns when ready to willingly transition to sinks for hand cleaning then tables for consumption avoiding resistant dragging. Repeat cue terminology — i.e. "snack time in 5 minutes friends, let's pickup".

Engaging Multiple Senses

Make eating enjoyable beyond sheer nourishment. Use colorfully printed laminated placemats secured to tables illustrating the foods about to be served providing visual stimulation generating anticipation. Name ingredients when directly serving plates teaching components. Play soft music establishing a welcoming atmosphere. Infuse rooms with scents of baking bread or pie crusts from toy kitchenettes to immerse senses and spark further interest. After meal times, have kids assist cleaning up by carrying dishes to tubs and wiping tables taking pride in responsibilities and achieving nurturing confidence.

Meeting state criteria for properly fueling kids while elevating engagement around foods through positive cues and consistent programming pays learning dividends also teaching healthy lifelong eating habits.

Technology Needs

Technology plays an important role in running an efficient and high-quality childcare program. As society becomes more reliant on technology in daily life, incorporating technology tools into childhood education environments has shown benefits for administration, teachers, parents, and children. This subchapter will outline key technology needs and best practices for childcare centers.

Administration & Management

Using technology for administrative and management tasks can streamline operations and paperwork for directors and owners. Here are some key tools to implement:

Child Care Management Software: Specialized software helps track enrollment, attendance, billing, accounting, meals, lesson planning, communications and more from one integrated system. Popular options include Procare, KidKare, HiMama, Kinderlime, Brightwheel and others designed specifically for childcare management. Features may include:

- Online parent enrollment and automated billing
- Classroom dashboards for daily attendance
- Meal/dietary restriction tracking
- Photo sharing between school and parents
- Push communications and mass notifications
- Built-in accounting, invoicing, payment processing
- Automated state reporting and form generation
- Student data reporting and analysis

Shared Cloud Storage: A cloud-based file sharing system gives teachers and administrators secure access to important center documentation and resources like handbooks, policies, forms, staff information, incident reports. Popular platforms like Google Drive or Dropbox allow accounts for each staff member with the ability to securely upload, search and find files across any device.

Surveillance/Access Systems: Security camera systems with remote monitoring ability allow directors to oversee multiple classrooms. Electronic door access control systems let staff enter via ID badges and allow centralized lockdowns. Some options also generate reports like timestamps of who enters and exits. High-quality cameras provide accountability and oversight for administrators when supervising staff and investigating incidents.

Payroll Software: Managing payroll in-house has many compliance rules. Using payroll software tailored for childcare centers lets you pay staff accurately and on time. Platforms like Paychex, Gusto or Quickbooks Payroll include tax tables for household employers and can integrate with other business systems. This prevents problems tracking and reporting employee wages, withholdings, insurance, retirement plans, PTO and expenses.

Classrooms

While technology should not overtake interpersonal learning during core preschool activities, teachers can thoughtfully incorporate tools to aid instruction and documentation:

Document Cameras - Also called visual presenters, these camera systems project images of documents, textbooks or 3D objects onto large screens or monitors. Teachers use them daily to enhance lessons with multimedia, highlight student work, or model step-by-step instructions.

Tablets - Certain education apps on tablets engage students in subjects like science, engineering, reading, math and social studies. Tablets also help non-verbal students communicate. Teachers assign specific apps for students to use independently or in groups that align to skills they are building.

Digital Portfolios - Creating an online portfolio for each child lets teachers document student growth with photos, videos, artwork or recordings. Teachers can generate progress reports faster by adding observations, assessments and examples of work. Shared securely, portfolios keep parents connected without extensive paperwork.

Music Players - Playing music during transitions, as signals (like clean up song) or during activities supports classroom flow. During downtime music helps relax students and reduces behavioral issues. Bluetooth speakers allow playing music from tablets without restricting device availability for other purposes.

Projectors and Displays - Installing wall mounted displays or projectors with screens facilitates whole class learning by projecting content in front of the room. Visual cues grab attention better than behavior correction. Smart displays also allow mirroring tablets to show student work.

Additional Technology

Further supplemental technology may be beneficial depending on program specifics:

- Smart light switches control classroom lighting scenes (like reading nook vs cleaning time)
- Noise monitors help teachers self-correct sound levels
- Video conferencing software enables meetings between parents abroad and teachers
- ID printers create secure access cards for parents and staff
- Digital sign-in kiosks avoid congestion during drop-off/pick-up times

As with any business processes, it helps to evaluate what technology can meaningfully enhance operations versus unnecessary gadgets. While childcare centers are ripe for innovation, balance screen time concerns with needs for accountability, communication and measurable progress between teachers, children and families. With so many choices now available, research options thoroughly, read user reviews, understand integrated solutions across platforms and carefully plan implementation training.

CHAPTER 6

MARKETING YOUR BUSINESS

Implement multifaceted community marketing across print, digital channels and partnerships to generate steady enrollment fueling your center's student base year-round. Dive into proven outreach tactics and communications for convincing prospective families to tour and enroll.

Website Development

A well-designed, informative website is a must-have for any modern childcare business. It serves as the digital entry point for parents discovering your services through online searches and word-of-mouth recommendations. Invest time upfront designing an effective website that conveys your offerings and builds trust in prospective families.

Follow these best practices when planning your childcare center's website:

Purchase a Custom Domain Name - Buy a domain name that matches your business name and brand. For example: littleblessingscarecenter.com. Options include .com, .biz, .school or regional domains. Avoid free generic domains provided by web hosting companies.

Create an About Page - Share your center's vision, values, philosophy, teaching approach and biography of the ownership/management. About pages build connection through your origin story and what sets your program apart.

List All Programs/Services Offered - Detail the specific childcare programs, curriculum style, safety policies and operational information. Common pages may cover daycare, preschool, after-school care, holiday care, summer camps. Specify ages groups served or special needs accommodations.

Facility Photos Gallery - Showcase your beautiful learning spaces with a photo gallery. Feature images of cheerful children learning and playing. Include captions describing activities happening in photos.

Staff Member Bios - Introduce the teachers, aides, cooks and directors through individual staff pages. Share experience, skills, education levels and personal hobbies to highlight their qualifications and humanize your team.

Testimonials - Sprinkle authentic parent reviews throughout your website and collect official testimonials from clients with permission. These endorsements address buyer concerns and shift visitors closer towards enrollment.

Online Contact Form - Include an inquiry form for questions which emails your center automatically. Respond promptly to demonstrate reliability. Offer phone, email, fax and in-person contact options.

Digital Brochures - Convert print brochures into downloadable PDFs. Reformat key info into web-friendly pages for easy reference by topic like admission policies, lunch menus, field trip highlights or summer camp registration.

Blog Subpage - Maintain an ongoing blog, event calendar or announcements page showcasing everyday activities. This content keeps parents engaged long after enrollment and informs the community of current happenings.

Visual Styling - Use a cheerful color scheme, balancing professional elements with playful fonts/imagery kids would enjoy. Ensure proper image resolutions and consistent branding across all webpages.

Mobile Responsiveness - With majority website traffic now via smartphones, use a mobile-friendly design adapting layouts/navigation for smaller screens. Test the interface on actual devices.

Building a custom site from scratch requires web development skills, but user-friendly DIY website builders like Wix or Squarespace offer drag-and-drop interfaces to create modern designs without coding. For best results, hire a professional web design firm specializing in early education clients to bring your vision to life with customized and conversion-focused features.

Plan to invest adequate time finalizing website content before launch. Proofread all text for typos, update photos annually and keep information current. Technical steps also include properly configuring email accounts, implementing security measures and facilitating domain transfers if switching providers.

Moving forward, actively maintain your online presence. Measure site traffic with analytics to see which pages attract audience interest over time. Keep iterating site content to boost engagement and search engine discoverability. With increasingly digital habits forming even among parents of youngsters, your website commands a pivotal role in generating new student enrollment leads critical for sustaining every childcare organization.

Social Media Presence

Social platforms present a major marketing opportunity for childcare businesses to connect with modern parents who actively use sites like Facebook and Instagram. Developing an engaging social media presence builds brand awareness, reinforces your center's childcare philosophy, and nurtures relationships with both prospective and current families.

Follow this primer to grow your audience and drive enrollment through social media:

Develop Business Accounts

Register official accounts on major networks like:

- Facebook Page (@LittleBlessingsAcademy)
- Instagram (@littleblessings_academy)
- YouTube (Little Blessings Academy)

Use clear profile images and cover photos reinforcing your brand. Complete descriptions summarizing center details, link your website and list location details.

Share Varied Content

Post a steady mix of content showcasing typical activities. Capture students' learning adventures to pique parent interest and bring your program to life virtually.

Photos: Upload themed albums like "Arts & Crafts Week" or "Winter Snow Day." Ask parents to sign annual photo releases.

Videos: Give quick video tours of classrooms, special programs or behind-the-scenes food prep. Short clips perform well to inform and entertain ideal future families.

Stories: Document daily moments through ephemeral Stories on Instagram or Facebook. Showcase special school visitors, projects or milestones.

Events: Create Facebook events for open houses, fundraisers, holiday performances allowing easy sharing. Live stream parts of events for remote audiences.

Articles: Pen helpful articles on early childhood development, profile influential staff, share summer activity ideas or holiday safety tips. Establish your expertise.

Hashtags: researching and using popular hashtags like #daycarelife, #preschool or your city name helps more users discover your content.

Engage Your Audience

Driving organic reach requires actively engaging your

growing community rather than just broadcasting one-way messages.

Reply to messages/comments - Direct message followers answering questions. Thank them for tagging your business.

Run social contests/giveaways - Increase exposure through user-generated content from fun prize competitions.

Ask questions - Take quick polls asking parents preferences for field trips, themes or menu changes.

Share User Content - Repost great photos or reviews from parents (with permission) to build credibility.

Interact with Groups/Pages - Comment on local parent group discussions referencing your program's offerings. Provide helpful answers establishing your school as a valued community resource.

Measure Performance

Analyze social media analytics like follower growth, engagement rates, clicks, and website referrals. See which content best resonates with fans to refine posting strategies over time.

Enhance with Paid Ads

Once your channels gain traction organically, explore paid promotional options. Geo-targeted Facebook/Instagram ads raise visibility further. Highly visual carousel ads perform well for driving sign-ups for summer camps or events.

Well-planned social media integration takes consistency over time but builds valuable mindshare through preferred information channels modern parents rely on daily. Humanize your center by giving fans a vibrant window into welcoming programs where their children can learn and grow.

Advertising Avenues

Beyond digital promotion through websites and social media, childcare businesses should explore advertising across traditional channels as well to reach local families.

Successfully advertising your program involves:

- Researching regional media options
- Creating effective messages/designs tailored to each format
- Establishing advertising budgets/schedules
- Measuring results and optimizing over time

This section overviews the most common and affordable advertising channels to consider when launching your first campaigns:

Local Newspapers

Local newspapers typically see decent readership among parents and families in your area. Take out display ads in community papers and parenting press showcasing your center's offerings.

- Submit various ad sizes/designs to test response
- Time ads to run near school registration periods
- Provide strong calls-to-action and contact info

Direct Mailers

Print full-color flyers, postcards or brochures to mail locally. Segment mailing lists by age groups and neighborhoods near your center.

- Promote new facilities, teachers or summer camps
- Offer limited-time discounts or coupon codes
- Include quick response codes to drive traffic to your site

Community Calendars

Get your open house dates, events and registration deadlines listed free on local media community calendars both online and their weekly print editions.

Billboards

Investing in a roadside billboard delivers high visibility, albeit an expensive ongoing cost. Consider splitting costs by co-marketing with complementary brands like tutoring centers, pediatricians or family photographers to share the space.

Vehicle Wraps

Completely wrap center-owned buses, vans and cars with custom artwork. Turn vehicles into moving advertisements viewed by pedestrians and other drivers when transporting students on daily commutes.

Sponsorships

Provide financial sponsorships and volunteer support to charities like children's hospitals, community fundraisers, little leagues and festivals. Negotiate branding benefits like t-shirts, banners and booth space to raise awareness of your center among attendees.

Welcome Packs

Assemble "Welcome to the Neighborhood" information packets. Introduce your center to new homeowners through real estate agents and property managers. Offer coupons to entice trial enrollment.

Waiting Room Marketing

Place professionally printed literature racks filled with your center brochures and flyers in high traffic medical offices. Prioritize OB/GYNs, pediatric clinics, imaging centers, etc.

Convention Booths

Rent expo booth space at major early education conferences, festivals and trade shows. Staff the booth to answer questions from educators and parents. Collect leads and giveaways driving traffic back to your site.

Radio Spots

30-second audio ads on popular local radio stations work well. Keep messaging friendly, benefit-focused and inclusive.

While each advertising method requires separate design, messaging and budgets, exploring a multimedia mix allows your center to penetrate the market across multiple channels.

Monitor response rates and fine tune efforts towards higher performing media for your neighborhood. Maintain advertising continuity to nurture prospects from initial awareness into converted admissions.

Partnerships with Companies/Agencies

Developing strategic partnerships with complementary businesses and agencies can expand a childcare center's visibility within communities while providing reciprocal value.

This section explores various partnership opportunities to consider and best practices for collaborating successfully:

Local Schools

- Approach nearby elementary schools suggesting after-school transportation partnerships for their students to your center
- Discuss priority placements for children of teachers and staff
- Explore classroom pen pal programs or reading buddy initiatives between age groups
- Rent booth space at their open houses and community fairs to meet families
- Seek guidance from principals and educators on ideal programming

Libraries

- Co-host family reading nights combining storytelling crafts and snacks
- Schedule weekly field trip outings for story hours and activity sessions
- Obtain passes offering discounts for families to sign up for library cards
- Ask about providing satellite classroom space for summer camps

Pediatricians

- Provide office waiting rooms with your program brochures
- Seek advice from doctors on health policies and resources
- Offer priority enrollment to their staff's kids
- Encourage doctors to personally recommend your center

Companies

- Contact local businesses to discuss childcare benefits for their workforce
- Provide discounts or reserved infant room slots for corporate parents
- See if companies will subsidize or reimburse childcare costs
- Ask about being featured in internal company communications
- Offer priority back-up care to their employees

Fitness Centers

- Partner with gyms to supervise kids while parents workout
- Rent space near activity rooms for pop-up classes
- Trade joint membership packages bundling both services
- Co-host events like Family Field Days

Retailers

- Ask grocers, toy stores or clothing boutiques about sponsoring onsite events in exchange for brand exposure to parents
- Negotiate mutual discounts for your families shopping at their stores

- Request display space for program flyers and sign-up sheets
- Explore joint giveaways like shopper bag stuffers during peak seasons

Freelancers

- Barter services with self-employed locals like photographers, DJs, magicians, or demonstrators to help at cost
- Trade childcare credits as payment for their contracted time

Aim for sustainable relationships centered on ongoing two-way value. While initial networking takes effort, the combined authority, endorsements, resources and exposure gained from aligning with respected partners pays dividends for promoting early education enrollment and parent retention overtime.

Ribbon Cutting Ceremony

Hosting an official ribbon cutting ceremony helps newly opened childcare centers celebrate launching their business with the local community. As an important milestone and photo-worthy media event, planning a lively, well-organized gathering can garner publicity and crucial word-of-mouth referrals.

Follow these best practices for orchestrating your own successful ribbon cutting:

Set the Guest List

Aim to attract around 50-100 attendees composed of:

- The Mayor/City Officials
- Licensing Agents
- State Representatives
- Neighboring Businesses/Partners
- Chamber of Commerce Leaders
- Tourism Bureau Directors

- Existing Families & Waitlisted Prospects
- Area Newspapers, Bloggers, Community Calendar Editors
- Friends/Family Members

Pick the Program

- Select an ideal date giving ample planning time that avoids conflicting community events
- Book an available official like the mayor or city councilmember to headline the event
- Print professional invitations and send digital invites listing full event details
- Prepare a commemorative oversized ribbon adorned with your school logo
- Order signs and vertical banners branded with your center name/motto
- Rent any necessary chairs, tables, sound equipment and decor
- Compile guest welcome bags or kids activity bags

Plan the Activities

- Schedule a 30-minute meet and greet prior for guests to network
- Have the owner give brief remarks expressing their vision and gratitude
- Invite the headlining official to say a few inspirational words
- Lead a round of applause then cue big ribbon cutting photo op!
- Allow time for mingling while enjoying light refreshments
- Offer tours showcasing classrooms and facility
- Consider face painting, balloon artists, photo booths or performances

- Raffle giveaways like free months of tuition credit

Promote the Event

- Send press releases to local reporters pitching great visuals
- Email parent ambassadors who can help spread the invite
- Post on social media and internal parent message boards
- Display posters around your center and on community boards
- Add a spotlight banner and details on your website

Document the Milestone

- Hire a professional photographer to capture candids during the event
- Collect B-roll video footage for future marketing
- Present commemorative ribbon cutting plaques to any VIP speakers
- Publish a press kit with photos shared online and sent to local papers

Ribbon cuttings mark grand openings with fanfare, media coverage and vital community connections. The public visibility, partnerships and enrollment leads formed will give your center momentum heading confidently into the years ahead as a treasured neighborhood institution for nurturing children.

CHAPTER 7

FINANCIAL MANAGEMENT

Managing center budgets, payroll, cash flow and financing options demands financial acumen scaling over time. Learn financial forecasts accurately, set pricing, handle taxes, comply with regulatory audits and monitor key ratios vital for achieving profitability.

Projecting Enrollment

Crafting accurate student enrollment projections is crucial for proper financial planning and success of any childcare business. Analyzing market demand to forecast both baseline target capacity along with realistic ramp-up periods allows owners to make sound decisions about staffing ratios, facility requirements, tuition rates and growth strategies.

Follow this comprehensive process when planning enrollment targets:

Evaluate Population Demographics

Study recent census data and community surveys to gauge key statistics like:

- Total number of families with children under age five in your designated area
- Birth rates over past decades to predict infant needs
- Ethnicity breakdowns to ensure cultural

competency
- Average household income ranges relative to tuition budgets
- Planned residential/commercial developments adding future families

Research Local Market Dynamics

Beyond raw population figures, research specifics around local childcare demand. Reach out to existing centers and preschool networks across all budgets to assess current enrollment levels, concentrations by age bracket, and number of students waitlisted.

Common dynamics influencing demand include:
- Working parent ratios needing full-time care
- Competition and saturation among existing providers
- State subsidization for lower income households
- Prevalent religious/cultural preferences
- Priority for high-caliber early education settings

Consider surveying parents directly at community events regarding their top frustrations finding care confirming target customer needs.

Define Maximum Capacity

Consult local licensing agencies to understand teacher-to-student ratio compliance requirements by age group for your target facility size and layout.

For example, a 2500 square foot center may accommodate:
- 1 teacher per 4 infants
- 1 teacher per 10 two-year-olds
- 1 teacher per 12 preschool kids

This would equate to housing around 124 total students at peak capacity spread appropriately across all programs.

Incorporate wiggle room for balancing classroom gender ratios as well which fluctuate year-to-year.

Map Phased Growth Timeline

Avoid the massive upfront investment required to open all classrooms immediately. Define an S-curve model that allows hitting profitability milestones incrementally:

- Phase 1: Open single infant and toddler rooms only
- Phase 2: Expand into preschool ages at lower teacher ratios
- Phase 3: Launch after-school programs using existing rooms

Conduct breakeven analysis to sustain lean initial staffing while ramping tuition revenue gradually over 24-36 months.

Forecast Enrollment Numbers

Compile data driving both enrollment volume projections and phase timelines.

Sample projections for a neighborhood center at 70% area demand could be:

- Year 1 - Enroll 6 infants, 12 toddlers
- Year 2 - Add 16 preschoolers
- Year 3 - Introduce 14 after school kids

Refine with Commitment Metrics

As your center's open date nears, monitor indicators foreshadowing actual enrollment momentum rather than hypothetical scenarios alone. Useful metrics include:

- Information session attendance
- Preschool application funnel conversion
- Deposits collected by age group
- Waitlists confirming interest

Continuously refine projections based on real-time commitment activity. While initially daunting, disciplined, data-oriented enrollment planning gives owners confidence for managing cash flow and making prudent investments for nurturing community children over the long-term.

Setting Rates Based on Expenses

Pricing programs profitably is an owner's greatest responsibility ensuring their childcare center can deliver quality education while sustaining operations long-term. Conduct careful cost analysis when calculating tuition rates factoring both business overhead and child-specific monthly expenses per age group.

Follow this process to set rates accurately aligned with expenditures:

Calculate Per-Child Costs

Account for direct monthly expenses tied to each enrolled student like:

- Meals
- Snacks
- Classroom supplies/crafts
- Portion of liability insurance per child
- Software licenses
- Nursing supplies
- Transportation fees

Establish average costs per toddler, preschooler and school-ager.

Analyze Operational Expenses

Beyond variable costs directly correlated with enrollment, incorporate overhead like:

- Rent
- Utilities
- Janitorial services
- Non-teaching staff payroll
- Accounting fees
- Marketing
- Loan interest

- Ongoing maintenance
- Taxes

Divide total monthly fixed costs across max classroom capacity for cost per seat.

Incorporate Salaries

Given employee wages represent 60-80% of expenditures, build rates factoring prevailing teacher pay rate benchmarks in your state.

Research ranges for Lead Teacher, Assistant Teacher and Aide hourly pay norms. Calculate subsequent annual payroll obligations per classroom factoring medical benefits and employment taxes.

Evaluate Competition

While expenses determine rate floors, also survey competitor tuition in neighboring towns evaluating comparables by program.

Set pricing keeping rates aligned to local perceptions of value across age groups. Adjust for differentiation like higher teacher credentials, newer facilities or more services.

Determine Revenue Targets

Combine desired profit margin goals with your prior expense analysis when setting rates.

For example, monthly infant care costs totaling $1200 per child would need to charge $1500 monthly to net a 20% margin, or $1700 monthly to achieve 40% profitability.

Communicate Rates Clearly

Present tuition sheets, discounts and clear billing policies to families upfront during enrollment. Highlight included amenities and savings through prepaid annual plans.

Proactively address affordability concerns certain parents may raise through flexible scheduling options, multi-child discounts or need-based financial assistance programs.

Revisit operating budgets quarterly, making modest rate adjustments where necessary while avoiding drastic spikes.

Keep rates accessible for existing families, while sustainable for maintaining program excellence families now expect.

Payroll

Handling payroll represents a mission-critical financial task for childcare centers as employer businesses. Owners must compensate teachers and staff fairly, while remaining rigorous managing payroll tax liabilities across federal, state and local agencies.

Follow proper protocols to process accurate, timely paychecks and required filings:

Choose a Payroll Provider

While payroll can be managed in-house manually, outsourcing to specialized providers streamlines compliance. Leading solutions like QuickBooks Payroll, Paychex or ADP integrate directly with your accounting system handling pay cycle calculations and deposits automatically based on hourly wages or annual salaries you enter for each employee.

Provider services include:

- Direct deposits into employee bank accounts
- Pay-as-you-go worker's comp payments
- Automated federal, state, and local tax withholding
- W-2 and 1099 form preparation
- Tax filing and payments on your behalf
- Payroll reporting and reconciliation

Classify Employees vs Contractors

Correctly categorize workers as official employees eligible for benefits vs independent contractors paid strictly hourly or per project without being on payroll. Misclassifying can risk IRS penalties. Review criteria around level of control, independence, full-time status and type of work when evaluating gray areas.

Track Hours

Ensure managers approve and submit hourly timesheets

each pay period for non-exempt staff like teachers' aides and cooks. Accurate hours drive net pay amounts and overtime wages if applicable. Consider time tracking software with ability to export hours directly into payroll platforms.

Enter Rates

For salaried directors, administrators and accountants, simply log annual salaries. For hourly employees, input their hourly pay rates, taking care to update for raises over time. Systematize saving rate tables for certain standard roles.

Pay Frequency

Set pay cycles based on worker preference and cash flow. Bi-weekly and semi-monthly schedules help workers budget better than single monthly checks.

Remit Taxes

Payroll providers automatically withdraw payroll taxes like Social Security, Medicare, federal and state income tax based on latest tax tables and employee form W-4 declarations for exemptions. Systems remit directly to proper agencies on your behalf.

Provide Pay Stubs

Employees receive pay stub documentation detailing gross wages, taxes withheld, reimbursements, 401K contributions, company health insurance costs and other deductions that influence net pay. Review stubs routinely for accuracy.

File Quarterlies

In addition to payroll tax payments, providers file required quarterly reports like:

- Federal Form 941 payroll summary
- States' quarterly employer returns
- State unemployment insurance tax forms
- Close Year-End

After year-end, employees receive annual W-2 earnings summaries for income tax filing. Contractors get 1099 forms stating non-employee compensation. Your provider transmits copies to the IRS and state departments as well.

While payroll processing adds complexity, non-negotiable compliance and relied-on income for staff depend on its careful administration. Choose a solution matching program size and integrate processes with vigilance.

Accounting and Budgeting

Robust accounting practices and disciplined budget management form the bedrock of financial health for any childcare business. Owners who invest upfront establishing orderly systems for tracking every dollar that flows through their center reap major benefits when leveraging data to calibrate operations, control costs and maximize profitability overtime.

This chapter outlines fundamental accounting and budgeting protocols owners should implement:

Choose an Accounting Platform

User-friendly software like QuickBooks helps owners manage full scope bookkeeping in a centralized database rather than error-prone manual spreadsheets. Cloud access allows remote viewing of cash balances, income statements, balance sheets, accounts payable/receivable and other ledgers to inform decisions.

Apply a Chart of Accounts

Create a standard chart of accounts tailored to childcare center finances, organizing transaction data into categories like:

- Income
- Labor Costs
- Supplies Expense
- Repairs & Maintenance
- Mortgage Interest
- Advertising
- Capital Expenditures

- Payroll Liabilities
- Retained Earnings

Track Daily Activity

Issue receipts for all cash and check payments from parents. Record daily sales, fees collected, reimbursements. Scan or upload expense receipts, vendor invoices, bank/credit statements to reconcile against ledger postings.

Inspect Statements

Review month-end profit & loss statements and balance sheets to understand emerging trends across revenue streams and overhead needs. Assess performance across key ratios like gross margin percentage or operating expenses as a percentage of income.

Establish Budgets

Set detailed, bottom-up budgets for upcoming year projecting best-case and worst-case enrollment scenarios. Estimate associated income as well as fixed plus variable costs quarter-by-quarter so actual results can be compared to expectations every period.

Pay Sales & Payroll Taxes

Confirm your accounting system is integrated properly with city/state sales tax filings and federal payroll tax payments through selected provider. Remit amounts due covering both employer and employee obligations.

Consider Audits

Larger centers may require yearly third-party financial audits with CPAs examining internal controls and financial reporting validity. Implement any recommendations that arise for bolstering integrity of accounts.

Secure Records

Back up digital accounting data regularly. Retain previous years' tax returns, receipts, canceled checks and legal/insurance documents securely on premises and via cloud archives.

Review KPIs

Schedule regular reviews of financial reports and key performance indicators with management. Adjust programs, rates or policies to improve metrics if certain departments underperform.

While intensive, consistent accounting accuracy and planning gives operators critical visibility that pays dividends managing payroll, measuring profitability and controlling unpredictable costs inevitable running schools.

Managing Cash Flow and Expenses

With slim profit margins common across childcare businesses, owners must vigilantly monitor operating cash flow and expenses to ensure adequate working capital sustains activities month-to-month.

Follow these financial oversight practices to maintain stability:

Analyze Cash Flow Cycles

Map typical timing and volume of major monthly cash inflows like tuition payments, program fees and rebates compared to large outflows like payroll, vendor bills, loans and taxes.

Anticipate potential lean months based on enrollment fluctuations, summer months or recurring peak expenditures. Proactively project and discuss gaps with your banking relationship manager.

Structure Payments Strategically

Offset bumpy cash flow by structuring parents' tuition due dates favorably on a 5th or 20th rather than 1st of months. This delays initial outlays for staff payroll already early in periods.

Incent recurring automatic payments from family bank accounts to improve reliability of intake.

Keep Receivables Current

Actively manage accounts receivable turnover. Print aging

reports detailing any outstanding family balances and timeline of last payment. Call parents promptly about past due amounts before sums grow large. Implement late fees consistently at defined thresholds.

Pay Down Debt

If carrying equipment loans or lines of credit, prioritize paying principal down faster whenever possible to limit ongoing interest charges draining cash flow. Consider debt consolidation options at lower rates.

Negotiate Vendor Terms

Approach suppliers about extended 30/60 day payment windows for large recurring purchase volumes. This flexibility helps manage episodic dips in operational balances between tuition installment due dates.

Build Savings

Aim to accumulate cash reserves equal to 2-3 months operating expenses as a contingency fund providing stability when facing enrollment fluctuations or emergencies.

Limit Excess CapEx

Carefully evaluate new capital equipment requests for necessity and ROI. Avoid overextending limited capital on non-essential upgrades. Consider buying gently used items.

Enforce Expense Oversight

Require managers submit purchase orders for approval prior to spending against budgets. Enforce limits on corporate credit card balances carried month-to-month. Audit expense line items for discretionary cuts.

Explore Financing

Monitor cash flow outlooks continuously. Have advisor references and paperwork ready for financing should the need arise to cover near-term obligations during tighter periods. Consistent cash flow vigilance and frugality sets businesses up to weather inevitable industry ups and downs.

CONCLUSION

Opening a thriving childcare business is a major undertaking filled with complex planning across legal, financial, marketing and instructional domains – but profoundly rewarding for those whose passion for early education drives their entrepreneurship. This concluding chapter summarizes key steps navigating the launch process and imparts final advice for aspiring owners.

Learn Licensing Rules: First understand federal, state and municipal regulations governing group care in your target region – from safety codes to staff background checks. Gain clarity on age grouping ratios, facility, meals and curriculum requirements applicable across nursery school ages and after-hours programs.

Conduct Market Research: Size up competition analyzing enrollment rates and perceived differentiation of existing providers before positioning your offerings. Survey area family demographics through census data and tap parent focus groups to validate demand gaps left by competitors. Quantify the addressable market's ability to support another entrant targeting various price points.

Secure Financing: With high startup costs, access funding – whether via small business loans, personal equity, or local grants/ incentives. Model multi-year income statement forecasts defining breakeven milestones across phased expansion. Prepare for dipping into reserves during the early student recruitment phase before achieving consistent enrollments.

Design Learning Spaces Beyond satisfying safety codes, create nurturing environments tailored to childhood developmental needs across classrooms, outdoor playgrounds and common areas fostering collaboration and growth mindsets. Blend active zones facilitating movement with cozy quiet spaces for focused work or reading.

Hire Experienced Staff: Recruit teachers and assistants exuding warmth, patience and self-awareness. Look beyond formal credentials seeking candidates emotionally equipped to form connections, defuse frustrations and instill kindness day-in day-out. Foster culture encouraging playfulness, empathy and diversity appreciation.

Structure Operational Systems: Plan daily schedules, family communication protocols and purchasing workflows recognizing the breadth of coordination childcare leadership teams juggle continuously. Arm administrators with capable child management software easing record-keeping. Explore catering, transportation and program partnerships proving more feasible for stretching limited internal bandwidth as student counts grow over time.

Market Relentlessly

With limited windows for securing each academic year's admissions, market continuously across digital, print and neighborhood settings. Host open houses for facility tours, document compelling social content from current parents, advertise enrollment ahead of seasonal decision cycles and distribute collateral to area "new baby" moms through pediatric networks.

Importance of Passion & Commitment

Certainly daunting on paper, owners powered by passion for positively impacting families through early childhood development thrive despite myriad complexities across legal, financial and interpersonal dimensions. View obstacles in licensing and enrollment simply as challenges to navigate rather than dealbreakers dissuading committed visionaries who understand their vital role. Appreciate and leverage the immense social returns possible from dedicating yourself to this calling.

Financial metrics alone provide insufficient lenses for evaluating the fruits of your efforts – spelled out in lifelong gifts of learning foundations forged in these impressionable years for shaping spirits and supplementing families each day. Allow the hugs and laughter filling your rooms sustain during periods of anxiety amid never-ending errands critical for compliance and solvency. Place balanced wellbeing for teachers and caregivers equal to budget targets knowing their energy engenders student outcomes above all else. Stand firm in your belief that prioritizing people fuels lasting positive change.

Final Thoughts

Childcare management demands extreme diligence balancing pageant regulatory, safety, emotional and interpersonal responsibilities while navigating market uncertainties. This playbook outlined key areas needing attention. Mastering the numerous competencies simultaneously poses challenges but unlocks social and financial returns outpacing other small business options. For determined owners aligned in mission to nourish infants through school-aged students holistically, the communities built prove profoundly gratifying, as both young learners and seasoned teachers continually broaden perspectives interacting under your guidance.

ABOUT THE AUTHOR

Amelia Thompson is an experienced educator and director who has successfully started and operated childcare businesses for over 20 years.

Amelia earned a Bachelor's degree in Early Childhood Education from the University of Michigan and a Master's in Educational Administration from Eastern Michigan University. She taught kindergarten and preschool for 5 years before opening her first licensed home daycare at age 25.

Amelia also serves on the board of her local childcare resource and referral association. She is passionate about supporting other providers in improving early childhood education access and quality.

Through her book **How to Start a Childcare Business**, Amelia shares the wealth of knowledge she has gained on starting and managing a rewarding childcare program from the ground up. When she's not busy working, you can find Amelia enjoying nature hikes, reading, or spending time with her husband, two kids, and golden retriever.